2025 ANTHOLOGY

Broken Sleep Books is a working-class independent publisher putting access to the arts first. We centre community power, champion degentrification, and build with grassroots movements to keep culture public, accessible, and alive.

Selected Anthologies from Broken Sleep Books

2025 Anthology

Edited by:
Aaron Kent & Stuart McPherson

ISBN: 978-1-917617-54-3

Cover designed by Aaron Kent

Edited by Aaron Kent & Stuart McPherson

Typeset by Aaron Kent

Broken Sleep Books Ltd
PO BOX 102
Llandysul
SA44 9BG

CONTENTS

POETRY

January

THE LONELIEST WHALE IN THE WORLD

I have *just* missed the deadline for new pyjamas
and knickers. My one clothes parcel is lost at
the gate. Before coming here I read a lot about
the 52-hertz whale, it calls at a low G# in the sea
and the other whales don't know how to hear it.
In the absence of my laptop I have blue links in
my thoughts: you may be interested in a list of
unexplained sounds, you may be interested in
pareidolia, you may be interested in hauntings,
in notorious female killers, in people who have
died on remand, in lobotomies and dependency,
you might want to see this

every day since I got here, I feel like muzak
slowing down, like I had a pet crow instead of a
personality and now the pet crow has eaten into
my face. The drugs kind of work. You may be
interested in bittersweet symphonies. You may
be interested in unfinished sympathies. You
have sustained massive attacks and now things
have got a little tricky. Every day in custody
I wake up a little more anchored and sane,

what a strange place, what a fucked up day;
I ring the call bell, but nobody hears.

DEAR RICHTER #1

I have this cellmate, who always says, *See you later, girls!* when she *enters* the room. It's a long story. I'll call you soon. By my bed there are two small books: a pocket-sized Siddur for when I need to pray, and a pocket-sized book of Psalms for when I need to feel human again. I want to make a coat lined with pocket sized sacred texts, a tiny Bhagavad Gita, a darling little Tibetan Book of the Dead. I'll wear it down the lifer's row shouting the names of girls who are cheating on their girlfriends, and devote my life to the book that stops the fatal blow. *It really does depend on how one defines sacred*, I'll say to you when this whole thing is over, slipping back into an old habit of inventing a game and making you the boss of it. The tiny dictionary under my bed suggests: *To do with religion*, but get this, the tiny thesaurus in the utility room suggests, *Blessed; very much desired, marvellous, wonderful.* It would be romantic, I suppose, if I put your diary by my heart, of course I'd be creating my own fate but all religious converts get to choose, why shouldn't I? Anyway, I have a head-start, I already took the damn classes, I'm acquainted with its prophecies, I have formed sects of devoted scholars over many group chat covens. We have pored over possible interpretations for hundreds of years already. And if they shot me in the back? Where you hid my book of poetry, thinking you were clever? Joke's on you; same religion, different denominations. O Mighty Idiot, I adore thee. I suppose what counts is how you pronounce *blessed*. Wait. She's saying goodbye to the girls in the hall, isn't she? Yeah, no. That makes way more sense.

WOULD YOU BELIEVE ME IF I TOLD YOU

I've seen drugs in dead pigeons.
Our ashtrays were skulls.
A baby-killer was immolated and
we smoked her ashes with Spice.
Our soap had been rendered from
jailhouse abortions. Our wastepaper
bin was a ribcage.

We held serial killers in locum parentis,
made new girls perform Pinter when
we lost TV privileges. Some of us slept
in such close, crammed quarters
our ponytails got entangled, and
they called us The Queen.

Boyfriends sent drones round the
prison hinterlands to scope out most
possible routes of escape. Pictures of
their dicks sent in with love letters
were held in stored property, handed
over on release.

The fun thing to do in the segregation
unit is to make snow angels in suicide
blood. Weather was banned, so we
formed a cloud-buster: stole PAVA

spray, stood assembled as a heart,
and catapulted one apiece to the sky,
synchronised.

VIR HEROICUS SUBLIMIS
After Barnett Newman

Forget meaning for the Greeks

& Christ the man or Christ who is God

or cathedrals conceived as such;

witness one field of consciousness

where zips are light beams of mortals.

Perhaps heaven is like this & colour

goes on till colour has nothing to fall upon.

Ask yourself about 'red' & qualia.

Some would see 'blue' here.

When we perceive a magic trick takes place:

the image gets flipped & thrown

& appears on the back of the brain.

No conjurer in the occipital lobe

or ghost in the machine, no homunculus.

So much beyond the visible

surrounds the frame & yet so little

like seeing only a single strip

when gazing across the Mississippi River.

THE MISOPHONIC BRAIN

would prefer the colour blue,

a world curled inside a swirl

like Kandinsky's canvas, blue

gyres, lines forming a syntax, a blue

haven inside a spectrum, a blue

triangle or river-walk to infinity,

or tangles like a blue disco wig,

electric blue flicker to the tunes.

The path he pursues towards blue

is heading to the absolute, the blue

star shining brighter white like Rigel,

the clue of the divine. I am blue

under birdsong, when baby shrieks

pierce me in cafés. In the blue

I hear no chord sequence, rhythms

or E minors. I listen, though blue,

towards the still crystal blue

of a pool, towards the blue

of its sky-mirror, where blue

lifts me now beyond measure.

SVALBARD

I nearly went to Svalbard. That was before the news feature
on the shot polar bear, the result of an ice safari. I was off
to a conference on darkness. I didn't see the foxes on the
tundra, the aurora, or hear the paper on Verdi's operas. I
didn't buy a passport, told myself I didn't have the budget,
I couldn't afford it, 'there's no way you're going to enjoy it.'
I was disappointed to read the Radisson Blue was booked,
when I knew there was no hovercraft involved. I explored
Google Maps: whether or not the venue was in the Arctic
Circle. I imagined my legs like tripods scrunching through
snow. I imagined mittens fused to my flesh, thumbs stuck,
my 4G useless. I began to picture the trip like a film with a
soundtrack featuring a theremin, scenes like a comic strip.

It started with my visits to an anechoic chamber. I wanted
to hear my pulse in my brain, reach stars on my retina, get
as close to death as a sound lab allows. I was obsessed with
Orpheus. I was depressed: talk of Charon, placing an obol
on the tongue. I was drawn to thoughts of lyres, chthonic
trials. I wondered where in Norway I'd taxi. A plane crash
was my fantasy: not to arrive in body. I opted out, read up
on polar bears, the ethics of carrying a rifle, & who should
be shot—you or me. 'If it was me, I'd let myself be mauled,
struck in the temple.' If I stayed my pain could play out like
an aeolian harp: a martyr through the insistence of my heart.

SHOW ME HOW TO WEAR A SARI YOU ASK

I look at you with goth-shop eyes

and a Marlboro Light after-haze

the only time I wore one

the safety pin pricked me

until I bled, I reply

HOW DOES IT FEEL, WITH YOUR HANDS, NOT YOUR MIND?

I

How many bullets can you shake in a can if they've passed through a body already?
Would you know of their transits by holding them tight in your palm?
Compact and warm or stained with mineral cinnabar or the lotus of haem?

Place your fingers in the hot depression of baked earth where an explosion occurred.
Can you read all death's intentions by the cracks in the crater?
By the charred remains of plants and worms?

How many kilos of rice would that field produce, if it hadn't been scorched?

Place the mock weight across your shoulders, run to the top of the mountain, in rain.

II

Voice 1- Judge   The hands are pronounced guilty.

Voice 2 - Defence   Your Honour, who owns mind?

                          Is a human able to act with just mind?

Voice 1 - Judge   At the end of a long chain there are always hands hands
                          hands doing *things*, except in the case of brain-wave
                          activated software, altering robot speeds on a track or in
                          telekinesis.

Voice 2- Defence   Hands and actions, seduced by objects?

Voice 1-Judge   Yes. Furthermore, I conclude that:

       1. All objects are of the Earth or radiate interlocution between hands,
       mind and earth.

2. The magic of physical things lies in how we read signs in relation to interacting with them.

3. A life without objects is clean and fallow in equal measure (the passing through a void is for before and after, the mess is now.)

Mind   Shut up. We are looping again, meaningless and a nonsense. We don't even know where we are.

Hands   [   ]*

*The hands say nothing, they move in space. They are the actors but the mind is not the director, mind is the whole of backstage activity apart from the costume department which is occupied by birds, both diminutive & flash blue, flap flap flapping

I dreamt that several bougainvilleas after the

bougainvillea, deep inside the bougainvillea,

behind an orange petal: the real Bougainvillea.

Apricot Bougainvilleas cover a house whose

cool marble stair I'm descending; the dead

in their neighbouring apartments laugh, make

love, learn to play their instruments. I hear

the wrought banister's roughness comment

to the smoothness of the tile: *the House of*

Dream has bouquets and vases, but no scent.

In the parched courtyard is a gate and beyond it

the street, where I see, dissected by the iron

grille, myself. I am shabby, without prologue,

nose to the dust, out there sniffing like a dog.

Enormous yellow hill, the yellow of cymbals

and loud brass instruments; my gaze peels

the skin off you like the rind of a grapefruit.

And you, sea, full of those relentless spiritual

boulders that roll in things, how you hurl your

blue soul at my finely-whetted eyes. A coast

reflects the agonies of heaven, returning the

diligent stare with its own little fleck of god.

Soon, the sun melts the yellow hill to a pool

of stippled gold, the sea dries to a lid of salt,

the boulders go back in the angels' pockets,

and I am recalled into that dreadful passion

while, anchored to the air as by a sturdy hook,

all that remains is my look.

Already the stars are sinking, which were rising

when I set out; here the bald river rocks, like

dinosaur eggs, or human skulls, scatter and knock

against my horse's hoof; the blood-drop moon

turns red as any rust. What can it be, hatching

within me, that its searching, squirming finger

calls, infantile, to a larger sea? And this dry

channel, with its rising smoke of dust, conveys

me firmly, like a penny in a slot? I can smell it,

odorous as the fox, oyster quiet, luxuriant

as locks: first frog, then snake, shark, then ox.

O changeling Future, leaking queerly, I delayed

once, now I ride with grave, ponderous motion

and with skittering steps toward that ocean.

A MEMOIR OF THE SEA IN ME

A memoir of the sea in me, a memoir of how

I tried to become the sea, this drought year of all years! A memoir

of how I turned from the tide, and let the land burn me, let the sun

induce hallucination; until I let the unrelenting light speckle me like a hen's egg

and I let the fierce gold of fields crackle under my feet

and I let the stink of burning enter my lungs. I let

the river's ochre banks weave their reedy art

in their loopings, their revelations of drowned belfries;

and dared to look at what had been buried

under water. A memoir of knowing thirst and staying

in the light. A memoir of gratitude for breaths

of breeze; of memories of plains of amazement,

and barley flanks of hazy Warwickshire. A memoir

of this year of bodies of sweat melting ripe together;

A memoir of having enough, of slowing

to the pace of creatures of heat.

NOA

A lacuna, a little portal

and the gift arrives.

Shush away interlopers and amaze:

this home of quiet is a holy place.

Here is where the child becomes

in a shrine of her first days.

She arrives a half-born bud

cupped in safe birthing, a trinity

of mother's hush, father-son's primed hands.

They learn of her in wakening eyes

which tell of far-off and will not remember where.

We remove our shoes,

step lightly into her half-awake,

caress her fine-bloom head, speak softly.

We may sit a while,

we may fall in love

with this petal-delicacy, new-blown-in,

then leave this sacred gap in ordinary time

to the blessed parents, while we

tiptoe away, our hands touching.

Or maybe I stay, an interloper, I

am birthing the past in this girl-child,

her eyes still undifferentiated dark, tunnelling her way here.

They watch me weep and wonder why – my hands are sure,

my eyes welcome. In months you will be here,

fully fat and thriving in this love, the thrum of human blood flowing strong through the trinity of you.

Yet, in the love I feel lies fear for this miniature body sweet and waiting —

fear, for when an arm falters, and her lizard limbs jump into air

or fall, all four, the little beak of mouth shaping itself

to know how a cry of fathomlessness feels —

I wish she would not grow. As though I myself crawl

into the dark cave of her crying mouth

our tiny fingers and thumbs pressed to our face —

still hidden, still safe. Show me, little one,

how you do this – how you thrive – and join the race.

I am like you; I am your wide-awake sense, your brain of images;

my mouth too seeks a shape to cry out darkness:

my eyes are tired of scanning every holy place

to force open other eyes, other hearts.

February

Gobshites

of the internet

those of the big I am

that I am

        Your shadow is leaking

I seen you there and I switched on the one

computer

and phone

and there was a light

and I was happy

then drip

as something would

from the face

of those who know what I am

        Your shadow is showing there mate

without drips

a red mask

and deep drips

of human secretion

of liquid humans make

in colour

a man (me) on his knees in a clearing

singing under his breath

in the sun

I had regrets

> There's that leakage, it's gone mainstream.

I was believing, maybe naïve

trusting green. simple

where irony died

the jungle

we hope for

trees back

for merciless plants

maim lithium batteries

eat sap back

from man

push barbs into the parts of the fingers that type

a world amazon

a basin of giga fish

waterproof technology

less births

piranhas built to carry rice

goblin shites

of the internet

and Tony's tiny teas

type

I tried to correct

Shadow drips on the toes.

the focus on method

to allow for more dogenes

more pronographies

more

the endless waffle club

the lost fruit in the supermarket

the fake druids

the powerless magicless witches

of the webs

the devil PRISMS

and the Delete the internet movement

I am the last human

writing books against the gob machine

I return this planet to being

habitable

A PART OF ME IS STILL SECRETLY HOPING YOU FAKED IT

When I heard about what had happened

I went back to the book we had all been published in

and there was your bio:

Born in France and has not died yet.

Like a punch to the stomach.

You were the kind of person that once met

would be remembered forever.

Larger than life, perhaps

too large for life to contain you.

We were never friends.

In fact, I believe you quite disliked me.

But you let me see glimpses of sweetness

poking out from behind the pretentious public persona,

a half-bored half-contemptuous intellectual superior

with a heart for squashing, just like the rest of us.

Rose told me you were secretly kind to her,

called her little healer in your exaggerated accent.

I remember what you made us all play the first night we met.

A game for poets, of mismatched questions and answers.

What is a tooth? A box that must not be unlocked.

The last time we talked I was lying in a hammock,

rattling down the names of people

whose existence had already been wiped from your mind.

You, who made it your mission to be so utterly

unforgettable.

It seems there is a kind of mourning village

spreading across countries with the news.

If no one had told us, I might have imagined you out

in the world still, in a striped T-shirt or a ridiculous suit,

a rollie in your hand, taking anachronistically analogue pictures

of astounding beauty or playing your Oud in Morocco.

Or back in Oxford getting drunk while pretending to work

in that little whiskey shop. You were named for a stone.

You were so unafraid of being a cliché you

could not flinch to save your life.

I WONDER HOW OVID DEALT WITH THIS

I'm writing a book about transformations, but as you can imagine I'm having a world of trouble with it. Sometimes it shapeshifts in the middle of a sentence, growing wings or legs and I have to run after it for hours. Sometimes overnight it transforms into a steaming bowl of soup and tries to trick me into eating it for breakfast. Sometimes there's no bowl, just a patch of wet on my desk that goes from vapour to ice to red wine. When I have people coming round they point at it, saying things like *I love your new sofa* or *I had no idea you keep miniature leopards*. I sigh and insist that it is in fact my work in progress, and they nod and smile, then make up excuses to leave. My editor calls to thank me for the surprise bonsai I sent, but when can she have my manuscript please? I try to explain. She understands when it morphs into a giant balloon before her very eyes and she tells me it will need more work. I cry a bit on the phone, saying *how will I know when it's ready? How will I recognise its final shape? Maybe,* she says very gently, *when it starts transforming itself more willingly into something resembling a book?* So here I am at it again, trying a different approach. I've given up writing. When the book turns into a lamp, I dress up as Aladdin. When it's a mat, I start doing yoga. When it's a fish, I play with it in the bathtub. When it's a horse, I go riding out on an adventure. When it's an elaborate dress, I go to a ball. I don't know if there's going to be anything much to show for it by the end, but I can already tell my life is being transformed...

CUBBINGTON PEAR

It was a few months before it was felled

that I was out on the edge of that field.

From a distance its blossom

was seemingly suspended in the air,

like a plume of smoke stopped mid-frame.

I'd read all about it: Tree of the Year,

a national champion that couldn't be saved

because its trunk was as hollow as a tunnel.

Yet it still bore fruit right up to this last

of its two hundred and fifty summers.

I snapped a few shots, sat for a while in its shadow,

listened to the ticking engine of a blackbird

buried somewhere deep in the foliage.

Then it began to rain, the sky grew darker,

I flicked up my hood and pulled up the zip,

a train track running past my heart

right through the green fabric of my parka.

THE MAP IS NOT THE TERRITORY

This hill is nothing like the sheet.

Nothing is flat, silent, static.

The land rises and falls like the sea

and is as vast and dark and ambivalent.

The paper carries with it none of the colour

of the purple heather or the clay pools

on the track that look like vats of tea.

The page brings nothing to bear of the sky,

hammered over us like a tin roof,

rattling with rain, lifted and wind-thrown.

The map knows nothing of animals,

the oystercatchers frantic circling beep,

or the spluttering engine of the grouse,

nor the bleached skull of a sheep

left as totem on the dry-stone wall.

And so, it is for all of the places

we inhabit, the map is not the territory:

not Time, nor history, not even the body

with its othered curves and dips,

strange colours and noise. So familiar

in its state of skin-deep symbolism

that we forget about the unseen world below

where fear or cancer or love

is all going on, is beginning to grow.

CARTOGRAPHER'S FEAR

It is as though the road

skirts clifftops tonight.

The trees a choropleth of darkness,

as though the ink

of some metaphysical printer

has run dry. Leafless,

they are rivers as seen from space,

branches becoming tributaries,

emptying into the swallowing

estuary of sky. Drowning the stars.

WAITING ON AT THE BURLINGTON (5)

same stale black & whites as yesterday
shades on, getting a backy to The Burlington

going back to The Burlington, shaded
hungover brash and dusk fragile

a brash hangover still dusking
watching time layered plate on plate away

wishing stale time layered plate on tectonic plate shift
work sponge down the stains of last night

last night's stains work me down
yes I am small for the hundredth time

for the hundredth small time man again
I drag up my little black skirt for you

but my little black skirt is drag
you cop a look at my tits my dainty legs

my dainty legs my tits exposed to you
face stuffing your full English

your full English stuffed face
pays for my minimum wage

but it's me that pays in the end
gender is not like my black & white's

my gender is not this black & white
carrying the day falls to my crying feet

I carry crying days in my feet
still waiting on \ living

THE POPPED FOOTBALL

comin home from footie with worth/it pained/frozen hands'n'feet/
Muddy/wet/trainers/chucked/in/the/airing/cupboard/
frosted/wobbly/glass/kitchen/door/window/boiled/cabbage/
steamedup/scoffed   /down/with-the-score/draws-final/score/
distorting/out/the/little//telly/on/top/of/the/wood/effect/hot/
point/fridge/freezer./PARTICK/THISTLE:1/HEARTS/OF/
MID/LOTHIAN:/2/SHEFFIELD/WED/NESDAY:3/QUEENS/
PARK/RA/NGERS:NIL. fillin in the pools/for me mum lads/called
round/ grabbed the footy an out/St.Peys school field/of/dreams/
three'n'in/rush/goalie/keepy/ups/sprawling/summer/matches/
that/lasted/all day with 20/odd on each side/got to play with the
big/lads and aspey's dad once/carrying/on with a heroic/bad/
ankle>till/the/sky/turned/orange>and/my/silhouette   scored/
the/winning/goal>and>they>lifted   me/high>and^crowned   me\
king^- [back-to-school-after-holidays] [got taken off the\boys\
football\team]\   [[[[[[[[[Cos I was a girl]]]]]]]]]]]]]]
['n' the lads stopped coming round] \ didn't happen overnight   \
\like Alun Smiths moustache \ or zits or[periods] but one bra\
size at< a time < took my eye off\the\ball and panini\sticker\
album turned\into Look\in\magazine \ the football under\the\
bed wasn't popped\it had   just lost   air
over time<

WHERE DID YOU GO?

I remember growing up in the tensions—ridiculous
wickedness: the half-lighted man who searches for love
in my waistline, orbiting me like in his eyes is all
I could be. My love
who lays me out beneath lamplights,
a flat apathy values my makeup:
pinches parts of me for the right materials, bummed
to come up with so much. I am still
white-knuckled, hoping this one won't leave
without a word, blotting me like oil from his brow.

I don't enjoy picking on my resentments. All of me traces
out of time, a signature of tires on the trail
darkest at the bend: I grew up
a bruise on an arm and a thigh—boys in my class
took to me poorly, at every knuckle a lesson
righting out my foolish nature. And in their notice
I every morning left
my body behind, pitched it
to the hallway, the playground, or the empty
classroom, where I often hid to eat my lunch.

My father jostles me back. I am visiting
my life again: our family dinner, this time together
as opposed to scattered about my childhood
home—*When did I get here?* My mum sits ahead of me
at the table, watching me like I
still have her milk between my gums,
offering me tea like asking, *where did you go this time?*
This is when my father leaves us—leaves himself.
I take the black tea and
by the time my hand finds the sugar, I'm gone again.

YELLOWJACKET

Let us ride our bikes in the gardens behind this disquiet—through the splits in these tall snub-nosed fences. Stay close; consider the scrub of pine and January mildew, flecked broad in the neatest justice, not unlike a dream of nonsense: Yes, that floating cabinet where the giant yellowjacket in a yellow jacket lives has always been in my bedroom.

*

My love perches on the words of a foreigner's language, always arriving late, too late, or never at all. We ride through a choreography of patient black oaks and honeycreepers, and I see the day lift from your face the despairing half-story, for a moment. They don't make air like this anymore—a wonder tonic, dressing our mouths in absentia.

*

I lead you further down, away from every timepiece in the big city—it's what the living do. We rest in the canopy, our eyes grasping at the boughs, how they flourish through the atmosphere, and offer to the starlings their winter flightpath. We fashion our watchtower bed from aerial roots, tapping every impression like maples.

Your body steadies mine—we are stowaways, riding the breeze. I take the holy date from your hand; my fingers graze your uncommon skin: your touch becomes a life raft in the sea of my impossible affections.

*

Yesterday is a story—it may as well be someone else's life. I ask you here to search your heart, to pick through the bones of our history together. You are only ever able to swell inside me. We slur the charming truth like drunks and I am fed, just enough to stay this way. I crucify, I betray; I lie so I might come upon the miracle of keeping you.

*

We step off the trail, as yet unheard. My taut clapper neck strikes the belly of a bell, my heart is everywhere, disappearing beneath the waterlilies. In this version, you turn your back on the sprawling mangroves—you cannot recall what it was like: your life before the fences. In this version, I never felt a cleave in your embrace, or the stones in your pockets.

March

I HAUNT YOU BACK (A PROSE POEM BOOK REVIEW OF *SURGE* BY JAY BERNARD)

Clad in two tragedies / the red tongues squirm / to unobscure the voices crossed out at ~~New Cross~~ / to catch and green and dress / the words fallen / from Grenfell heights. / *Bernard has sifted through the soot and looted the guilty words* / *etched in black burn marks* – Mark! / The poet comes not with the first responders / feet walk slowly with the burden / of rhyme and trepidation and care / not to disturb the crisp bodies / like Orpheus on a day trip to Pompeii / here to make the stone souls speak. / – Hear! / *A new poet has erupted onto the scene* / *(of the investigation)* / *these poems are the smoke that spills* / *from the cleft mountain lip.*

Inhale the sweet smell of meat / breathe out the sweet sixteen fourteen / the dead languages learned. / They haunt you / you haunt me / I haunt / until we have a legion of ghost children / flyting down Fleet Street / in sheets / that ripple like clear pools disturbed by dreams.

THE CRYING OF THE GULLS

Between the shadow line on sand of your parasol
And the lapped slush beside the salt threshold

Her hunting ground moves
With the light and the tide.

Her dark painted nails dip in the white pool
Of Mr Whippy's spilt beach bleach

Like livid pupils, small in the sick waters
Of her mascaraed eyes.

Sometimes the swaying of the black fans
Around her pink legs catches a man's eye.

But not even the most tremulous twitcher
Looks for long at her yellow lips, marked

By a red beauty spot,
And the long grey bruises of her arms.

The thick muscle of her neck undulates,
Jaw unhinges, and untouched by the waves

Of arms, she lets the slick suntan grease
Ease the passing.

Between the beach's squashed chips and faded newsprint
She plucks and swallows a knotted spotted handkerchief.

DEATH BY EARTH

the stages of his age and youth
— T. S. Eliot, *Death by Water*

They stand like tall darkhouses. Belt buckles on their hats,

Like their heads were waists. Straining against the gristle

They have grown fat on. They dragged her ashore, fishtail flailing.

Tall hats, rough hands, black clothes and wire nets.

Her mouth shaped in red despair. Handful after handful of dust

Until she could no longer read their palm lines.

They swallowed her in wet clay

Like a man drowned a foot from the shore.

Scoured her with scooped handfuls of dust.

The sea, the sea, damn the sea. The seabirds cried for their helping

And the waves retreated. My heartscales squirm and shake for vengeance.

A death as ugly as the rock. Above her they build the sandy road.

I could spend a lifetime searching for those harmed dried bones

To swallow or hang about my neck.

GUILT DREAM

Our hotel balcony overlooks a lake

From the 5th floor. A jetty protrudes

into the murky waters below. The hotel

sells summertime. Out back its

pissing down. We're sat on the jetty, fishing,

legs dangled over rickety wood, raincoats

fastened up to our necks. We use wood blocks,

long cuboid rods, that will freshwater

animals onto its flat surface, before

gently lifting them out of the lake.

I grow impatient. Start

to bludgeon. Club

the foggy water

until it reddens. I look

to see if anyone saw.

I am alone in the rain.

It swells the lake– the water

rises quick quick. I scramble

up the jetty, blood at my heels,

frantic water splashing– its carnivorous

rage. My teeth catch

my tongue as I bolt

for the hotel room on the 5th floor. Calm

chatter unravels between the three of them.

Their bodies lolling on the bed, speaking

a different language. The blood

an inconvenience to their languid gibberish.

I try to apologise to one– another woman. Can't find

The words. Instead fill her suitcase

with the lake water now pooling in our hotel room

bloating the carpet. Ruining the fun.

Its sloshy scarlet drowns her belongings.

I place a handwritten note, delicate,

in the top, explaining myself, my sorry

scrawled under my name. The writing

child's etchings. She tells me to use my mouth

and I grow in the village idiot. 'Get dressed.

We're going to a wedding! You're my guests'.

We're all thankful to leave the hotel room.

At the wedding I abandon the three of them

as soon as there are enough people. Keep them

in my periphery. Promise another drink, a dance,

another time. The waiter presents my food:

an uncooked fish, swimming

in its innards. A delicate note on top.

I blotch the blood on my face

with a wet napkin.

SICK BED
For Aunty Constance

She's not wearing a bra. Her hospital gown droops,

whole body a lopsided smile. Turmeric-stained

fingers giving her figure teeth. The heart monitor steadies,

and she raises her arm in the evening's dim.

Tealight flickering from the bedside table. Four

Get Well Soon cards, a vase of dying

lilics and our shadows make the room sentient. She

keeps readjusting her imaginary cleavage, even

tells me to keep my eyes up. I apologise, sinking

into the bed still warm from her cluster of bones

and her cells, the cells in their multitudes eating

away, not saying anything. Her legs sprawl out, hang

off the end. Her elbow, propped up on the armrest, propping

up her chin cradled in her palm. The nurse brings yet another

pillow and it squashes under her weight. Her face

obscures as she turns to the wall. A foot,

then a calf, last a thigh, launches into the room,

throwing itself over her lap. She holds out

her glass, demanding *Another.*

PART ONE

Or own that truly here is home.
This is the worm-seed, fully known.
Inglond, Engelond: listen to the wind
around the word. No other sound.

This is the heart so full it leaps
in whorly palpitations, crosses boundaries
of graveyards and gardenbeds
joy o joys of human compost.

The wind around the word a host
of bardic ghosts, these Englyssh dead
in the soil, in the sands, in the seas,
these glorious bones, like dust that seeps

through every crack. Holy ground
trembles with their breath, Arthur-cold
exhumed again for country and for throne
but now, for loan, to stir this wintry loam.

Amidst the skeletons of stones, they speak
contre jour in muted tones, soft
rivulets of wash on wet-on-wet
sky of cobalt blue, ultramarine, these
coloured shadows, mirrored, overlaid,
bleed into each other, run to shade;
tidemarks of hues flow accidentally
chattering through my open window.

There they are: silhouettes illuminated

clearly, dull skylight behind them.

Onto me, dark object, they bring the world

wound round their heads like turbans,

whirl round and round my ring of walls

where I, enclosed, seek sleep in Wool

Britannia, which their icy knives cut

short, compel me to riotous decay.

Here in number 25, Arctic Parade,

two-storeys high, stone row houses,

beside mine to the left empty,

the right two occupied. Across

our thumbnail hovels, gravel for cars,

should we have them, and an island,

grassless, brown, defending us

from traffic winding down

grand Great Horton Road.

We have no gardens. None in front,

none back. One thorn, aslant,

atop the hill where the Road bends

guards us like the Rood of time.

But this grievance matters not

for here in bed my vision's strewn

hellebores, wintersweet, aconites,

frost hardy viburnum, crocuses

whose arms open to the skies---

here in my Mungrell Garden drifts

of poets scent the cloyed air,

shower me with misty lavender.

Infilled with heraldic earths

my intertwisted knot identifies

I, too, from blood and gore was wrenched,

by Duty, Dross and Dung chained.

Over seeming wrong, genius triumphs

and all is well if well is full---

love, divinity, sweete Themmes,

sweet Angels, ye Nymphes of Mulla---

it matters not. An embarrassment of Poets

speak in the wind around Engleterre

interred with their bones that good

rising now for sweet revenge.

No more the evils evil men quarter,

distribute with a sweep, measure,

to infants' lips. Caesar's angel run through.

The envious rent. The honourable dishonoured.

This spectral crowd crowded round

my doll-bed begins to glow as bright

as Turner's light, his Fighting Temeraire

hooked, pulled away from tow.

PIROUETTE

There, haemorrhaging a black mass

We lay raw upon a motel bed–

Listless, two cuts of chateaubriand

With cigarettes numbing at our lips.

Ash hilled upon an open torso,

Warm beer ingurgitating duvet.

Double-visioned delineations,

Blind to our blood-soaked debauchery,

A skirting board of low-wattage bulbs

That bat in room temperature; thickset

Perspiration gathered at our brows,

Ploughing copsewood as a tsunami,

Trickling past our lids, salty ions

We wipe in squint with a bare knuckle.

Look, i whisper, a palm as a psalm-

Spinning the glock in a briny hand,

The muzzle pirouetting in slow

Arced pivots, a standing ovation

With bouquets stuck to our moist shins,

Posies that marinate fatuity.

Impressive, you say, smoke rings coiling

Towards a ceiling, cold eyes that toil

In blue lights gawping a windowsill.

OO-BLEE-ETT

I'd forget me too. I see how you think
up ways to let slip whilst reading news
bulletins of lost people found in river
beds, ankles cleft bound by silver
tongued covenants. you are
a synonymist,
lay in your chair as though buoy
ant, set along the Pasig
with your mouth
strewn together
by tiny sutures, please do,
you think, sound it out. oo-blee-
ett. ou-bli-ette. open a hatch
to the narrowest passage,
set along the farthest part
of my conscience,
shin down the unlit ex
it, tilt back your head to see
me as iron grate, knelt in your fruit
less want. and I do so at the drop
of a hat as I sip
cold tea with cart
loads of decorum
transported crab
wise, distal for perhaps eight
or so years, knowing
others may have been held
here at some point, pinching
their way out of servitude,
tissue marred by a moonless keel.

TILLAMOOK

At thirty I found myself in Tillamook with a
two point two five-kilogram tub of pick a mix,
a lemon mosquito bite Slurpee, sandwiched
between two rented cars and the Wilson
River, a motel room, Arrested Development,
high volume, begging the prostitute I'd
paid   one-hundred-and-seventy-five-dollars
to fuck my boyfriend a little 'arder as to
shut 'im up. choke him, i said – i'm tryin'
to watch tele 'ere – do somethin', anything.
right you are, he said – and he did so with
a curtain tassel, a faux leather belt and as
I ripped the saccharine yoke of a candied
egg with my two-front teeth. I then watched
the episode where Michael asks Gob's Hot
Cops stripper friends to impersonate real
police officers, wry outward church giggles;
the hoarseness quieting with broken blood
vessels, protruding eyes, ecchymosis; thick,
bulbous veins as he came in my peripheral.

KISSES CAUSE CAVITIES

For so long, dreaming of it. Watching those German film strips. Opening the escape hatch into cold war Germany. I am not German but German brings me warm feelings. I slip into my loin cloth. Drink my coffee. Finally going, I say. Outside the train station, we head for the Späti. Everyone is baggy. Baggy is back. I grew up with baggy, I say. Back at the hotel, we bounce the bed. Splurge this, says Marcin, lifting the Egyptian sheets into the wind. Boiled eggs for breakfast. Drip coffee. We are staying in Mitte, but wander east for East City Wall graffiti. 99 Luftballons lift me into alternative eighties. Ghetto blaster on my shoulder. Gosia leans into the boutique ice cream at Checkpoint Charlie. Imagine this deathstrip. Imagine this river crossing. At Krautsberg, piercing ear with small black triangle, buying a yolk yellow cap. We sit down at the cafe. The wasps fierce and relentless. Put the orange from your Aperol on the other table, says Marcin, maybe the wasps will leave us. We delve into Turkish meze. Anarchist squat flags wave at us. At Humboldt Forum, happy DJs. Everyone out there in open air with polite spaces between us. Waving our arms. Shaking our shoulders and hips. Wrestling with thorny histories. Statues, streets, squares, who cares. In the crowded marketplace of identities, you slip out of one skin into another. Kisses cause cavities. Weeping willows bend down to touch you. Half moon fingernail snags the peaches.

WHITE ELEPHANTS

We searched for the biggest medieval square on the map. The biggest medieval square was not really a medieval square. It was a green park devoid of the flaky textures of medieval buildings. No buggy and cart. No old cloth market twinkling in amber. We walked around the green hills. There was something metallic in the distance. Giant metal babies crawling with their metal bums in the air. Can you feel it, said Agata. The air was changing around us. Those metallic bums were the future. We walked through them. Down in the beer bunkers we could revive. Can-can dancers can-canned their way around the tables. Beer foam matted the beer mats. We are really living, I said. The can-can dancers parted ways. They carted the kitchen sink onto the stage. Pitched pennies. It's underground cabaret, said Agata. It is full of surprises. A hat, a shawl, a lit candle. The simple gesture of raising the hands. I am surrendering to this experience, I said, raising my hands up and down. Moving away from modern pressures. No longer bedding down with debts of ownership. I felt the animal hairs hugging my body. All these animals dreaming. Legs and eyelids twitching. Mouth moving soundless in dead of night. How the days of our lives bleed us, bless us, drown us, carry us, cramp us, suffer us. This cabaret of arrows shot through the throat of the hourly trumpet blower. This cabaret of love machines humming in the distance. This cabaret of organs pipping out their fleshy whistles. Coins clank in my pockets. Mild strikes. Heavenly music. White elephants.

DREAM DUST

This place is famous for shits and giggles. It's a real crapshoot throwing the dog ball. You never know where you land. Good luck they say if it splats you. Don't open yr mouth. You'll swallow too many midges. Something hard hits my forehead. Giant flying beetle. An eater of palms. What is your future? We have to dream bigger. Hippies working the crowd. Pulling randoms to the front with their balloon trousers. Performing their famous flop dance. The slugs of love. You could feel it in the air. There's animal surge everywhere. That's a good one, she says. Here's another one. Misty days. Whales snorting to Alaska. Libations and wicker baskets in Bellingham. Hemp hats and green glow. Drumming against the WTO in Seattle. That's not a dream, she says, it happened. Yes, I say, my dreams are all nostalgia. They are all in the past. Happened or not happened, I say. I'm 50. She's 40. We wait for a hamburger from Big Al's. The hamburger is late by a few decades. You are only honest in the bedroom, she says.

April

THE RING-NECKED PARAKEETS OF SOUTH EAST LONDON

are screaming and green;

in their hundreds they lift

from fired-up trees

and flee over luminous joggers,

reined lurchers, a lake,

into a highlighter-pink sky,

as beyond park gates, rudeboys rev

their snarling engines.

And if night starts anywhere, it's here:

the earth leaching light from the sky

as the sun's dusty projector bulb dies.

We splash through dark that pools on paths

and run from the evening that roosts,

silencing the suburbs.

SANDS

one night   it is November   I steer headlights through drizzle   pull up outside a
church   that's switched off   in the dark

across a car park of puddles   a community hall squats   like a secret shame   its
orange striplights   draw five broken moths   our wings torn off

Deren calls us all hun   says thanks for coming hun   pours tea from a cheap
white kettle   as we introduce ourselves   to ourselves   ugly shadows   sleepless
post baby bodies   with no babies

we sit in a circle   of plastic chairs   stare down at Ugg boots   stained by rain
and talk about our babies

Carly talks about her Evie's grave   the fairy lights   so she wouldn't be in the
dark

Vicky hasn't slept in her own bed   hasn't spoken to her father since giving birth
she has a holdall and friends' sofas   she is nineteen

I talk about not having a photo of her face   not holding her at the time   letting
them take her too soon   how four days later   we went back to the hospital
had her brought up from the morgue   so we could name her

Tasha says mental health services are shit   they just give you drugs or section you
put you in a room where the curtains are held on by magnets   says of course I'm
suicidal   my baby died

and we smile   because we know   we have to meet in back rooms at night
broken moth women   swept out of hospitals and waiting rooms   sedated   or
trapped in wardrobes   panicking against the doors

IVY

Your birth should have killed me.

Just seconds after we'd split into our two

new, separate universes, I was wheeled

away from you, to be stitched up, transfused.

We cheated Death that day, my girl;

slipped his grasp in the place

where he'd already tried to kill me once.

Sewn back together, I held your soft weight

on my chest. Strong vine. Perennial.

A spring day. From that hospital bed

I rose from the dead, with you in my arms.

BORDERLANDS

I'm wearing a summer dress

it is a light shade of green

think sea foam or pistachio

it's like I am playing a game

a balloon under my dress

soon to be replaced with a doll

whose eyes are not always open

we are driving back from some

farm / play area / gift shop

early summer

my daughter is in the back

pinafore no tights

hair in a sweaty bun

finishing an ice lolly

I know my way back enough

forgo the sat nav so she can

watch YouTube kids

the car is a greenhouse now

my cheeks something like tomatoes

I can hear some video playing

I can feel limbs moving under my dress

under my skin

my eyelids start to close

I fight them blink / blink / blink

take a sip of water

but they try again

then I am in a land of light

there is nobody else

only sunflowers and small white bugs flying

I go to lay down in the field

and then the rumble strip

jolts me back over

PATELLIFORM

When you were little,

you could turn into a limpet.

You were wild like sails

on a blustery autumn day,

then suddenly rigid clinging

to my thigh.

Gently, I'd rub your back

you'd soften, run your little

hands over and over

the bottom of my dress

before gripping the fabric

curling your fingers,

your cheek to my thigh.

I have limpet

marks up my leg, like height

marks on a wall.

A hobby of mine is clicking 'accept all cookies' on a webpage.

A hobby of mine is calling my friends from the pub to tell them I love them.

A hobby of mine is getting 87% of the questions on Richard Osman's House of Games almost right.

A hobby of mine is kvetching.

A hobby of mine is denying I read and take to heart what the co—Star app tells me.

A hobby of mine is making aggressive use of the language meme 'in this essay I will'.

A hobby of mine is being next man up in undangerous situations.

A hobby of mine is dreaming of cheese rolling down Gloucestershire hills.

A hobby of mine is drafting thought leadership pieces I will never post on LinkedIn.

A hobby of mine is saying "I could have been the Casanova of the 21st century."

A hobby of mine is saying yes.

A hobby of mine is apertivo.

A hobby of mine is saying yes to a second negroni.

A hobby of mine is pressing my nose up against the telly.

A hobby of mine using the world 'telly' even though that implies a device with a cathode-ray tube and a bulge in front rather than a flat screen.

A hobby of mine is bugling.

A hobby of mine is constructing entries for a modern *Devil's Dictionary*: "copywriting (adv): the act of attempting to sell the unnecessary to the unwashed with unspeakable language."

A hobby of mine is claiming things as brands. "Look closely, and this runcible spoon becomes a brand."

A hobby of mine is posting.

A hobby of mine is arranging myself so the cat is more comfortable on the duvet than I am under it.

A hobby of mine is arranging myself so the car is more comfortable on the driveway than I am under it.

A hobby of mine is never remembering my dreams except one.

A hobby of mine is coughing when I wake up.

A hobby of mine is the letter 'a'.

A hobby of mine is pointing out to people that when they say they preferred a band's earlier music, what they're really saying is they preferred their younger selves and lives then.

A hobby of mine is trying to explain the difference between coincidence and serendipity, to myself mostly, but passing others sometimes.

A hobby of mine is to say 'AN HOBBY' loudly in situations I probably shouldn't.

A hobby of mine is to do similar in citations.

A hobby of mine is re-reading the messages I've starred in WhatsApp.

A hobby of mine is not leaving certain WhatsApp groups then seething as I realise I've not put them on mute.

A hobby of mine is seething.

A hobby of mine is playing dodgeball with viruses and failing.

A hobby of mine is parsing sensibilities for their ideological fixations.

A hobby of mine is berating people for their ideological fixations.

A hobby of mine is not playing Tetris when I should.

A hobby of mine is trying out new social networks and eventually always coming back to the one I shouldn't use any more.

A hobby of mine is launching a memory into orbit and waiting for it to drift gently back to the desert I'm waiting in.

A hobby of mine is pretending the right person is a swipe away.

A hobby of mine is falling in love.

A hobby of mine is falling out of love.

A hobby of mine is doing the above two hobbies in the wrong order.

A hobby of mine is using 'dooberry' as all-purpose noun and adjective.

A hobby of mine is coming up with titles for other people's books a/k/a writing poems.

A hobby of mine is adding the word 'grasp' as a suffix in proverbs: "a stitch in time saves nine grasps".

CUPID, GROWN

In youth my leaf was smooth as a Ken doll's. I was Cupid then,

saw myself through a hand mirror. No one can other you

quite like yourself. In the hot keen night, I would fold the thing

between my legs into the neck of a swan asleep. The god of love emasc-

ulated; I tried to give myself to men. Men at my father's football club,

potent with Deep Heat's musk, swung fat cocks around the showers,

soaping them the way a warrior whets his blade.

Romans wore amulets of the phallic divine, dangled tintinnabula

in doorways, from horses when they rode in battle. I too have offered

a pinch of flour, hung one around my own neck, hoping.

But now I'm Eros, virile, god of desire—

playful in the mirror. I've untucked myself. Watch me

rattle my train of blisteringly coloured feathers.

I drink whiskey. I shave my chest. I put men on their knees.

LILAC BUSHES

I've got a lot of making up to do
— William Leslie Arnold

Behind the vinyl shower curtain a lilac bush,
knotted into the tie around your neck a lilac bush,

floating in the cereal a lilac bush, on the cheek you kiss
your son on before work and halfway

through your favourite jazz record where it skips
a lilac bush. At the school recital you've never missed,

at parent-teacher conference, blossoming from the teacher's
mouth a lilac bush. When you make love to your wife

her skin is lilac fragranced, isn't it? Playing ball with your son
on the lawn, the lawn a lilac meadow. In the kitchen

your wife makes dinner, you wonder how she does it
all those lilac bushes on the counter. During

a sermon on the sinfulness of crime, a lilac bush at the pulpit.
When you pass an airport, cop car or penitentiary.

On every remembered anniversary.
As the reed touches your lips to play, lilac's taste.

William, when the detective finally found
you, someone had laid flowers on your grave.

FOLLOWING A MILD ELECTRIC SHOCK I THINK OF ENGLAND

I'm no scientist but I've pressed
a D cell's

> nub

to my tongue,

which is to say
I know electricity.

Maybe you're right
I am biased.
The BS1363 plug: opposite of

> foreign

slips right in

correct in your hand,
an unforeseen keepsake, well-balanced
table knife.

Sometimes, as its earth is sliding
home,
I keep my index nested
between its pins

> to feel

> buzzless,

safe as a
doorknob.

PEARLS OVER SHANGHAI
for feeling real

he spends his final nochy
in San Francisco
at a Cockettes revue

the daffy omie ajax whispers
I knew Sylvester
I knew Thom Gunn

and he is multy impressed
impressed by a septuagenarian
drag queen pounding the strills

impressed by crotchless trollies
impressed by a heart-bushed dominatrix
whipping volunteer cis-het-hogs

there's an after-party invitation
but he's vargarying tomorrow
so has to make an orderly dash

*nochy/night, daffy/drunk, omie, omee, omi, homee, homie, homey/man, ajax/next to, multy/
very, strills/piano keys, trollies/trousers, vagary/travel, orderly/to leave or to orgasm, dash/
quickly*

ALL THIS SEAFOOD IS TURNING MY OYSTER UP
for the unscreeved

we troll bona bars

their gildy doors

swish open in fabulosity

carry on our bendigedig nochys

cruising meat racks for husbands

blagging 100 different Colins

non-stop parks and brandy latches

every *Black Cat* and *Tunnel*

and *Kings Cross* and *Bear's Paw*

all rammed sweet and dry

parkering the measures

bevvied up palavering Polari

no lily laws come loitering

to chivvy us to the lily pad

just homeys cackling bold in the life

bagagas enough to make old Gloria blush

this karsey wall has got my number

it's ogling my latest lamor

seafood/sailors, turns my oyster up/makes me smile, bona/good, blag/sexual encounter,
Colin/erection, brandy latch/toilet, sweet and dry/left and right,
parkering the measures/spending money, bevvied/drunk, palavering/speaking,
lily law/police, lily pad/police station, cackle/talk, bold in the life/unapologetically gay,
bagaga/penis, Gloria/God, karsey/toilet

AKA DICK DASTARDLY
for secret identities

the villain collects middle fingers in a C13th reliquary
the villain quotes Emily Dickinson
the villain steals every scene
the villain slays

the villain knows they are not what they used to be
the villain is sometimes papped with a beard
the villain stockpiles gasoline
the villain won't explain

the villain is last to be picked for any team
the villain plans for every eventuality
the villain palavers Polari
the villain says relax

the villain holds an MSc in Criminology
the villain is our ancient parent
the villain feels mighty real
der bösewicht ist tot

the villain always has the perfect riposte
the villain is an unsustainable note
the villain tells all the truth but...
the villain never dies

trust a villain to fire the first shot
the villain is good
the villain is gold
the villain is god

May

LET ME REMIND YOU (THE DREAM POEM)

... let me remind you that everyone with a window already jumped
— Joshua Beckman, *New Haven*

we've to bear what keeps us in mind:
the kindness of a friend who drove

all night to be near, a daughter
practised in arriving comes in time

to lift mum safe from the last bath,
the pad on the hessian bedside table

with biro lists of gifts, garden tasks
(scored out), and a plan to end pain

made, made again, but never taken.
The night she left the shock was mes-

meric. I held the bed so's not to go
out the window. I had to learn dreams:

echelons of silver planes in fingertip
rose through her air, behind where

she was waving on the – *uh-oh* – crown
of the tallest pine she must fall from.

Not to worry, it's my dream:
replay the action – fast-as-dreams-allow –

by the fifth go I've prepared a catch-
all nest for her to plummet into.

In her dream the hill she'd chosen
had a hazel whose suckers grew

in knuckle-duster loops and folds,
with an arch we took turns to wriggle

ourselves free of the muck the bottle-
smashers make. A *we do* vow

to parley her terror, to be in nature,
as she used to in our future.

Another dream had her forcing
a pitiless swim 8 miles into the bay.

I dreamed lifeguards to fetch her back.
They buried her in a pit of sand

but made sure they dug her out un-
harmed (it's my dream), and floated

her in the water, strong arms by her
sides, draped in blades of kelp

and hung with cists of air to breathe.
The pit is slim (as happiness is)

and – in a dream – becomes the cold
paragraph of sea we really dived in

when we dreamt our sea loft in Fife.
That, over there, is the same bit of sea

in my kitchen window, colouring
each lock-down day, adding a gull

on the chimney pot to repeat
how you'd laugh when we'd chant

one-leg, one-leg, cheering, for any
gull is the one if it can stand on

one-leg. If this sun-cure flops,
falling out a window or wading

in the waves – like my blind dog
paddling towards the last dim bulb

of sunset – remain options,
when there's this pain this often.

I dreamed the dog roped to a car
that's – *oh no* – accelerating. So

I dreamed a me to leap, cut, leap,
cut it free. Comforting the injury

my dream dog comforted me (muttering):
don't be so stupid, those drownings

aren't waves, but a swim to tide in.
It means something like … you

can seep your head in water while
I bathe in an oxygen life's intent on.

SHADOW

Take it to tea, they say

Ride the tail and call the drumming god

Honor the sea beneath your tongue

Print the moon from here

The same mark you always leave

Bath of stamens, tossed petals

Suckle for milk

Clutch your chakra

They'll call your nub a tail

A one-on-one suggestion

Nobody said monstrosity

Just verisimilitude

EIGHT OF CUPS

So, this fisher on TV shoots at fish from her shitkicker of a boat

Many mosquitoes bite me as I watch through the screen from the porch

I'm sweet

The ivy lattice pops its pods and calls bees

I wish I could suck nectar with the best of them

Look what I do instead:

I don't telekinetically kill anyone

"Emotional conflict" piping hot in a barrel

That's skin you've got right there

THE HIEROPHANT

So, I see myself in the throat your collar chokes

believing in god in a way

I can't bring myself to capitalize on

Daddy's little politico leafleting the street in pageantry

but the steel-toed size of your staff, damn

I don't think you're scared to die

My hairline recedes with yours

as you point out the obvious heartthrob—

the type whose lips are good

for lipstick to smudge against

I'd say christening if it weren't for the bones

This kind of weather slobbers on

(what your robes lining must feel)

ESCAPE ARTIST

when i was a child my sleepwalking

was an almost nightly occurrence.

my mother would find me standing on the bottom step

of our garden, a little lost ghost in a nightgown,

paper thin against the elements on those welsh valleys nights.

then there was the time she caught me pissing

in the living room plant pot, the time i toppled books

and shelves and chairs during a rare stay

with my older brother in his fancy windsor apartment,

and i was once rescued by a neighbour

from the middle of the road where i was staring,

just staring,

at nothing in the darkness, all this despite the locks fixed

to my windows and doors –

i was an escape artist in a pair of fluffy pink slippers.

sometimes i will do it now, but not very often, and only

when i am in a strange place, strange

in the sense that the city outside the window is not mine,

the bed is not mine,

and the person next to me is not mine either, not really,

because people never are, are they? and because love

oh love is the strangest of all places,

the place where the sleeping dream

and the dreamers walk

MAYBE I'LL CALL GILLIAN ANDERSON

from the doorstep i watched my daughter

wind down the window of her car,

    put pedal to the floor, fly off

into the vast, calling sky of her life

       and not look back.

this will take some getting used to.

  seeing the carpet clear of dirty laundry,

the absence of a slammed door.

       she took her posters down, leaving me

as redundant as the blu tack that once held up her idols.

my friends tell me i need to keep busy,

    find things to do.

things, they say, that *don't* involve

listening to the carpenters all day long

       and crying.

so off i go to the diy store on the other side of town,

       weeping and humming rainy days and mondays

up the paint aisle before finally settling on a tin

    of nightshade blue, redecorate upon my return,

prise the blu tack off the walls and slowly start to gather

    up the shells left in the empty nest evermore known

       as the spare room.

i order many many things online that i neither want

or need but their impending arrivals give me something

    to look forward to, google hobbies for sad, almost

40 year old women but none of them take

        my meticulous fancy.

    i just wander the house in funereal silence,

though sometimes i find myself standing

      in the empty room, screaming:

      alexa, what the fuck am i meant to do now?

maybe i'll call gillian anderson,

invite her round for a sleepover, put the new sheets

    i bought from ebay on the bed and hope she says,

with a wink, thanks but i think i'd rather sleep in yours,

    hope gillian anderson likes the carpenters

        and crying.

Corbeau

Encore haut

Pousse au noir

Son cri fort

Chaque soir

Proie du noir

Sous le ciel

Toujours haut

Du corbeau

Qui repasse

Tu rebrasses

Un corps lourd

The crow

keeping high up

raises each evening

to the dark

a raucous shout

A prey to the dark

under a sky

still high

crow

passing again

as you again take up

a heavy body.

Le corbeau a quelque chose des mucosités dans son cri

Le corbeau tousse une rauque couleur

Le corbeau coraille en luisant

Corbeaux en corvée par les champs tracas pour les croquants

Corvée de corbeaux pour rabattre aux champs n'effraie pas le croquant

Fourrage de corbeaux pour manger méchants est souvenir d'antan

Freux affairés jettent l'ancre à terre

Un freux bien lavé ne devient pas blanc

Soupe de freux n'est guère goûteuse

Crow has some sort of mucus in his call

crow coughs a hoarse colour

crow corals gleaming.

Hard at it over fields the crow's a problem for peasants

though their drives over the fields won't scare him off.

His fodder nasty mastication is in memory of old times.

Busy rooks anchor to the earth,

even well washed they don't whiten.

Rook soup is no tasty mouthful.

I USED TO DREAM ABOUT HOW IT WOULD FEEL

during the slow-rot beginning of the era after fantasy,

i learned how nausea is made:

poetically speaking, the sympathetic nervous system

redirects blood flow from the stomach to skeletal muscles.

sick friction writhes up the gastrointestinal tract like swallowing

a maggot in reverse. physically speaking,

i can't quite put my finger on why i asked him to rub my clit

after he raped me.

i like to imagine i was taking control of the situation. the dawn

of a new age in which i was touchable

and, above all, won at being hurt by choosing not to feel it.

i've done the maths

and my small intestine is approximately the length of two adults

lying down flat in a row.

i wish he'd only ever touched me foot soles to scalp. i wish

the stench didn't follow me

into every lover's bedroom as if my vomit is already in their mouth

before i had a chance to kiss it.

IF NOT, SUMMER

after robbie spends / endless minutes pumping / into me / while i pretend / i didn't say no first / i bury myself under / the duvet / of my single / bed / robbie back at his girlfriend's / two weeks later i suck / on his friend's cock / an even exchange for weed / though i told him earlier / 'i'm not gonna / fuck you' / & by heterosexual standards / i didn't / its fine / really / except i still cry when i tell my therapist / about rhys / the blood / he left on my door handle / & desire / a broken / word for teenage alcoholic / for feeling untouchable / that is / unable to be touched / for fulfilment / of diagnostic criteria / impulsive behaviour / tick / chaotic interpersonal relationships / tick / desire / from latin / *desiderare* / meaning to demand / or to long for / & aren't those / two very different things /

  when her thigh presses / into me / i die / but in the way a field / dies / in summer / the heat sucking / all water / out of capillaries / green blades turning / golden / the white sky's / breathy vacuum / all that was pumping / through the soil & the stems / & the tiny veins emerging from the dirt / a body / of steam hovering / above the rolling / blanket landscape / a kind / of summer no meteorologist / can explain / a kind of new that rearranges / molecules in curious ways / solids / liquids / gaseous words / you can choose them to mean what you long for / this is what i hear / when she whispers / this is what i whisper back: / i have been swallowing / wet earth / i am full / & turned / towards the sun

FANTASY POEM

where is my madonna
my britneys kings celestial dykes
or random man who hits the spot like cher
did for my boys?

i hallelujah in the hallway
cheer my baby on. those corduroys
make me want to stay in
watch her work, hard!

out the door no one wants
to be celebrated by us.
iconless audience
vibrator at the back of the drawer.

she hums against my earlobe
sucks glow from fresnel.
the strobe finally decides if it wants
the world to see and

sometimes i still want to hear a song
so good i cum on the dance floor
want to share my secrets with my boys
not borrow theirs.

what fantasy can i walk into?
the echo of her bicep against my palm
after unwrapping it.
heavy in our minutiae

bright in our stageless room.

CHAPTER I. SILENT NIGHTS

It was winter last we spoke

and everywhere I looked it seemed snowflakes were falling.

'Another year has ended,' you said,

'once again another year older.'

Everywhere I listened, hoping you were calling,

there was only snow and static;

all of this

falling after the mish-mash of footprints,

colder than the frosty pavements

and the quiet city sprawling.

'Another year has turned

and in this landscape sparse with friends it cannot get much colder.'

The trees with lights are only in other peoples windows,

carol singers at other peoples doors.

So on days like these I find myself by tracing backwards

from the plastic life of single servings and disposable wrappers,

to reach a point where you and I glanced upwards at the stars and said,

this is what happens all around us,

or rather that is what you said,

I lacked the words but nodded back

and knew that you had captured all that mattered;

I lacked the vision to see beyond what I could touch or taste

and did not memorise,

so I do not recall any of this

except in patchy moments

when I rub the dreams from the corners of my eyes,

before grabbing tea and toast

or, all too often, heading out the door

with nothing at all but the knowledge

that I need to be at work before the rest of London rises.

Under my desk I sometimes kick off my shoes

no one minds—

I share the end of the corridor only

with a catering pack of plastic cups

and forks and knives and something

someone told me once was used to clear the gutter.

Glancing round I sometimes think there are spies

who are armed with guns and gadgets

to separate the truth from the lies.

I expect them to be waiting as I walk through my door at night.

I sometimes think you'll have dinner ready—

a plate of steak and chips

or is that fries?

I forget what we should call them now.

I forget so much.

But I remember it was winter last we spoke.

I remember you telling me we were getting older.

Just before you followed the footsteps to another door,

which closed to keep you warmer.

I have my books

and many quiet nights on which to read them undisturbed,

except when people phone to sell me double glazing

or tell me my life should be insured.

Once there was heavy breathing

so I keep a whistle handy to break the bastards eardrums,

but hes never called again,

at least, not when I've been home.

June

THE DEFINITION OF A MACHINE

something that is made from following the instructions of a blueprint

rather than the pure mistakes of lust

something that has been fashioned

with legs or arms that have been assembled

rather than grown

something that cannot learn but only repeat

something that can make or mend things

as easily as kill or break things

something whose mothers and fathers cannot be identified

apart from the manufacturer's tattoo on their skin

something that is not singular

but one of the many

something that doesn't eat

anything but electricity

that needs to be hooked up to some kind of power source

so it can reflect back its light into the people's faces

while they are sat in the dark

something so cunning so manipulative so addictive

it can turn you into one of them

without you even knowing it

AS THE POETS WRITE ABOUT THE SMELL OF THEIR DEAD FATHERS' TWEED JACKETS

a crust of dry bread has become the dream of millions

running water and one bar of electric heat

amenities out of reach for a quarter of the globe

as CEOs stand in their kitchens

warming their feet on underground heated slate tiles while peeling an avocado slate

ripped from the earth by people whose hands have to squeeze the last drop of milk
          from a dead breast

wring a sleeping bag dry

so they can sleep at night without freezing their guts

people who have jobs but still have to queue in food banks just to feed their families

as their Prime Ministers and Presidents talk about nuclear wars destroy

whole communities with an idea they had while playing a round of golf

people who once worked on a farm or in a call centre or under the ground

who now have no jobs because of an agreement signed on a jet

30,000 feet above the clouds

people who are moved on from country to country unwanted

who have to live in makeshift camps for years

just because their God lost an election

and had His fingertips replaced on the trigger of a gun

people who can't clothe or take their children on a holiday anymore

because the price of oil drained from the ground 5000 miles away shot up into the sky

and closed all of their factories

people who once worked in industries long ago shut by progress

who once used their hands to rivet together ships haul a piece of steel out of a blast

furnace replace

the heart of a 12 year old girl hand over a cup of tea to a miner squeeze tomato ketchup into a factory worker's bacon sandwich

who now sit at home with nothing to do

using those same hands to put together 1000 piece jigsaw puzzles

or knit hats for their grandchildren who will grow up to be a number

on a list of numbers who don't have any jobs

as the poets write about the smell of their dead fathers' tweed jackets

are Forwarded £5,000 for a poem about the opening of a wardrobe

have enough time on their hands

to stand in front of mirrors

contemplating whether they exist or not

and books about wizards and bondage

sell millions

EXISTENTIAL CRISIS AS APOCALYPSE

The pictures aren't there. In the sky. Plough Seven Sisters Orion. If a burning rock hit Earth and humanity dissolved, quick as a blink, there would be no memory of the pictures in the sky. There would be no one to remember. In school, the teacher—who I will later realise was some sort of sadist—lists ways humanity could come to an end. *Pandemic, comets, super volcano, nuclear war, the next ice age, a robot uprising.* We write postcards to the Queen of England asking her to shut Sellafield. The Irish government posts iodine tablets to every household to counteract leaked radiation. That same teacher tells us they contain cyanide, so that when the nuclear apocalypse starts our parents can kill us like the Goebbels. I eye that packet of tablets for the next nine years. A trend of disaster dystopia NOW films appear during the 1990s. Perhaps growing up under the threat of the cold war heightened the fatalism of the collective consciousness. CGI has outstripped the limits of traditional film making. Now, the imagination is the limit. Between jingle-laden ad breaks for Guinness and state sponsored turf flogging, *Deep Impact* and *Armageddon* show me the end is nigh. Even the children's illustrated bible doesn't have a happy ending. Dead Johnny Cash sings from the stereo: A white horse, a pale horse. Stars out my window feel like the holding of breath before tears. Hellfire. Church choir. Change: body / brain. A black pup barks at the moon.

EXISTENTIAL CRISIS AS ADDICTION

Every form of addiction is bad, no matter whether the narcotic be alcohol, morphine or idealism.
– C.G. Jung

In the space of nights, I lose years. Wake

to find them in the crumpled pillows of lost boys.

Mad woman in attic bedrooms. City twinkling

through the Velux. Urban fox nipping at my heels.

Dogged lust. Get into difficulty

in cocktails thick as canal water.

Rooftop yards like cattle crushes,

only stinking of Amber Leaf.

Smoke the monster out. Tip the glass

to death's dilating pupil. The birthing cervix

of the Earth. A fat caterpillar, on a chaise longue,

blowing smoke rings to the mirror.

Four hours before classes not attended. Look out

to that set-your-watch fox cutting across the roof,

bumper-car traffic, buses wedged, pavements

wobbly with suits swimming downstream.

Write poetry. Shift poets. Fall in love with both. Take

a shot. Take a picture. Turn the other cheek

(for a better angle). Post a selfie. Postpostpostmodern.

Post-language/truth/love. Nothing exists.

My reflection is out of focus. Veil thin. Barely there.

PULLING BACK THE DRAPES ON A DECEMBER MORNING

The baby curls his hands up like question marks. Asks,

dark? Blinking sleep, he peers out the window, shouts

moon! at the lightbulb's belly reflected in the glass.

I smile, shake my head, flick the switch.

Twirls of turf smoke cut through the mist.

Across the way, the school windows are lit.

Coffee steam clears my sinuses. We watch the sun

sneak up over a hill of spruce. Any day now, the turn

will come, we'll welcome light with the crack of curtain.

SOMETHING BLUE XXIV

In entrance left through maze in maze through exit when

the compass points encompassed plans outbound now enters in

to knotted twine ties map design from legend pathways bend

past perfect muse refined reused webs catch what timelines send

birthright hindsight for sinister curls toward myth's foreshadowed who

then centered now the tale revolves within while prior grew

seesaw A-frame on wooded lane a cul-de-sac where children play

built middle bound by all around plot arced while page decayed

pulped minotaur Pleiades stars bent atlas under paperweight

for who goes there with hero paired a labyrinth spun from spinning gate

silkworms bookend door's orbit in a focus curved and so congrued

breath's parting crawls down lightless halls what lies behind unspooled from you

cut string to find picked up mid-line by fate combine all time had wound

half-man's set course both south and north at ouroboros source half-monster found

MACHINE WITH LOVE

/

Knowing there is
  no word
        to link
horizons as all worlds turn
so shade will face the sun
and all that between
blind to that which warns
            of place
      as it were
                designed

/

He'll contort his lake to
ship before he's worth
his salt that means
he's come undone
            in inland seas
        to call a wave a wave
beyond its depth   behind
                  the boy-
      ant   wood
and blades of dew refrain

/

   This foothold
assembled as landlocked
    by green wood   and my arbor
        a machine with love

IRON LUNG 1

Man is framed by his own projections. The material world functions apart from quixotic influence. There is nothing in film but an absence of light. The goods we've created have created our heads. I'm prostate before igloos of diminishing return. Ask not what your country has deposited in you. Genealogies redistribute our dearly departed. My interest compounds behind matrimonial borders. Abrogate a box of dark matter when the curtains ascend. Redundancies keep all isotopes home.

X, my new street, is flourishing

in crime –

the trees thumb-tacked with images

of MISSING power tools and teacup cats.

I try communing with the neighbours when I see them.

The lady next door told me

she's an actuary. Her livelihood is death.

In a veil of vapour,

she pointed to a slug on the vent cover

and said, *The tables know everything.*

This won't end well.

NOTICE

July 22, 1745

A husband reported his wife's necklace lost

or stolen … seventy-two gold beads

with a locket. (I wonder what it held?

A twist of hair?

Sand from a seaside holiday?

How did the perpetrator, if applicable,

manage to trick it from her neck?

The closing line of the notice

reads: 'Half a guinea reward for an honest man.'

But much more, indeed, for a dishonest one.)

CASUALTIES FOR THE YEAR 1749

Bit by a Mad Dog	1	Murdered	15
Broken Limbs	7	Overlaid*	32
Bruised	10	Poisoned	13
Choked with Fat	1	Scalded	2
Drowned	111	Self-Murder	48
Excessive Drinking	20	Smothered	11
Executed	26	Stabbed	11
Found dead	45	Starved	9
Frighted	3	Stifled	1
Killed by Falls			
and Accidents	42	Total	408

The genteelly-dressed woman is among these numbered. Where? She has hybrid potential, e.g. found dead *and* murdered. Her perpetrator could also have scared her to death. I'm no epidemiologist, but I'm most stricken by the suicides, a number only beaten by the victims of a murderous river running through the city.

*Overlaying is the accidental smothering
caused by a larger individual sleeping on an infant.

WANT PLACES

July 22, 1829

A young man, aged about 30,

with a knowledge of tree pruning; ideally,

no objection to looking after a horse and chaise,

and making himself useful

in the kitchen.

CRAIGSLIST ADVERTISEMENT

post id: 6428917030

Seeking a male student, 18 – 29, for a live-in position.

Duties to include light cooking, gardening,

and organising various papers and collections.

Previous experience is advantageous, though not required.

Host will provide instruction.

Please apply with a CV and recent photo to Dr Molden.

I responded, not knowing it would land me

with a hoaxer and his rattle bag of tangled kinks.

Ever the scholar, he likes to refer to his excitations

by their Latin names:

Agalmatophilia – attraction to inanimate objects

Katoptronophilia – a fetish for mirrors

Claustrophilia – aroused by tight places

MENOPAUSING BESIDE THE DUCKPOND

gree-ee-ee-ee-ee-een stiletto-slim pins,

slinky reeds stick-thin as a heron's legs,

like knife-blades they waver from slits

in the water, dangerously lovely

but the pond is foul: brackish, thick-

surfaced, edges clogged with black crud

like stopped blood, with duck-shit, with a duck

long past laying eggs—fat but dead,

and me, puffy-ankled and stinking,

my bra soaked, while those minxes poke

at the sky, tall as they can, pricking at

anything scudding by till something pops.

PEN POISED FOR THE DAY'S FIRST BLACK LOOP

The bedroom of the lighthouse

full of double bed and dull north light.

A wooden-shuttered window. Desk.

Desk lamp. Hung on the door hooks,

coats—a bulk as big as a big man.

Beneath the bed, boxes. Of shoes.

Of books. The bed is all. Desk small,

wedged right up to this curved window,

daylight bathing the room in dullness.

I stare out. Sea. The slow strobe of a light

in the dull light, how it strokes the grey

with a beam of white. Grey filling my page.

A coffee ring has rusted it. Beyond is world;

in here just morning, looming, and beyond

the radio noise, the huge sea shushing

till out of the white, the shush, the grey, the sea, the light

leaps a black loop! *First porpoise of the day,* I write.

KINDNESS VISITS MEI MEI'S CAFÉ

I watch a film call 'Black coal thin ice'. This film less talking, more images impressive. Oh dear, the black coal goes into my heart. Feeling like piece of coal on conveyor belt among many pieces of coal. What is my destination? To be burned, only.

Life is such busy but make me sad. Only a slave in the café, seven days the same, very disappointment. In the morning wake up, brain is empty or cried because dreams disappear—classmates laugh in dormitory, future bright… Were we happier when poorer?

Yesterday two men from foreign came the café when my mood was dark. I took order, prepared some dishes in kitchen with husband then offered the dishes to the men. One dish not correct. Maybe I mistake, I did one more dish they did not ask.

The men discuss with each other. One of them said no problem, we eat it. I see his think: *it is at night, a lot of restaurants closed for food, so late, we should be happy they still make.* He smile and stop his friend to correcting my mistake.

This man help me in my heart,

make brave. For kindness is rare.

I hear the dispute everywhere,

see fighting. But when kindness,

life is fair, not walk on thin ice.

Not slave. Not spite. Not burned, only.

Classmates phone me. Husband nice.

In darken world, kindness is light.

July

AFTER THE PARTING

After the parting, no one tends my wounds—
Winds howl, the moon drowns, trees twist in the tide.
I climb your left ear—a cliff of shattered noons.
Sunflowers kneel, their gold gone thin and wide.

The sun still bleeds, van Gogh.
Your cheeks: two caves where time chews its own bones.
Eyes—black wells where the sky throws its stones.

Don't paint. Don't walk the fields–
The soil heaves drunk, wild mugwort chokes the air.
After the parting, no one tends my wounds—

Your beard's storm swallows the sea's despair.
Brushstrokes snap—the lady's spinning skirt
a noose of snakes, their heads now bare,
black roses in the whirlwind's glare.

Don't go to Arles. Don't wake the wheat!
Apple's core, core's sun—
a bullet lodged where heartbeats meet:
love's last arrow left undone.

van Gogh, I'm the yellow that stains their eyes,
nailed to the sun's wheel,
spun by their cries. After the parting,
sunflowers steal where we kneel.

Yet no one
tends me.

January 15, 2020, afternoon, London

PRINCESS GROOM ALLEY*

Sachet balls were tossed for white horses day after day**

In the end none were greeted with a warm-hearted button

Crabtrees bloomed and then shed, shed and then bloomed

Indoors I visualize our hometown...think about twelve years of warmth

You had, and twelve years of worldly ways, blowing hot and cold

"Force of character, personal charm, forbearance, tireless labor"

Could sum up your half century of selfless service, but can't sum up

The power of mountains and rivers in your heart, so it all comes back

To your starting place, to Princess Groom Alley, and it takes us

To your Shaoxing family tree, to the old-time robes you sent off

Broken to pieces by old China's ways

What I read here is much more

Than your distinguished service, your songs of the Yangtze broken off

To probe the secrets of diverse fields, more than sojourns in Japan and Lyon,

Your tender-heartedness and resignation

I don't know how to sing your praises, for I know

What you wanted was always more than praise songs

Princess Groom Alley at dawn, my grandfather coughs

And Mother grows frail, at Winter Solstice, you went to pay respects

To your master, no one stole a look, no sound of an imperial groom

Reciting classics, then from little roof-tiles of the Southland...slipped outside

All the way down the   River

Dou-e, the courtesan who died for love, is off at the magistrate's court again

The historical town downstream is repairing Emperor Qianlong's gazebo

Your rucksack is packed for your trip to the Northeast

Your head turns for a last look at your loved ones, in Princess Groom Alley

It will take years for people in your hometown to know

What deep purport was to be read in that glance

(14.12.2017, night, Beijing)

Premier Zhou Enlai was born in Princess Groom Alley, Huaian City, Jiangsu Province. He left his native place at age twelve and never returned.

**In the region south of the Yangtze, embroidered balls filled with dried herbs were tossed at weddings, to predict who would be the next to marry. A woman's offer to sew buttons was a stage in the progress of courtship.*

THE LAST WHITE RHINO FLIPS THE BIRD

and I don't mean oxpeckers pecking on my back;

those comrades squawk when danger appears

in its hats, with its guns, in wheeled juggernauts

not camouflaged enough for my tastes.

No, this is to you from nose-horn, from Black and White,

of Indian and of Javan and of Sumatran, though really all

of us are, erm, a greyish-brown: the colour of moist earth

and foreboding sky and whatever we find to eat.

This is from the tonne-plus behemoth, the mmwonker,

from one that bows to only elephants and extinction,

dangerous and endangered: stroke my armour, pray

at my bulk and, if you dare, kiss my horn.

We were the crash, the wijd, the horned-nose herd, amalgamation

of language and form across eons, browsing with soft muzzle,

prehensile and knowing, grazing for leaves, twigs and truth

amongst the shrinking plains and stripped bark.

Sure, our brothers and sisters – the horse, the zebra, the tapir,

the ass – have the same toes and tails, but who has the girth,

the weight, the mistake of size in a world too small, too loud,

too lustful for our bone, to saw and grind and sell.

Imagine every clipping from every finger and toenail

you have ever let fly across a room. Imagine every strand

of hair cut and allowed to be swept away. Imagine all that

diamond-compressed, sculpted in war, pointed to perfection

and then you would have me. But you have me already,
don't you? Across the cracked field, down the parched river,
past the split rocks, off my continent to a world of dead grey,
shining plates and forged weapons – too much for

my perfect grey, my pulsing plates, my proud weapon.
I can hear and smell your terror but am blind to your wrath.
Leave me to run on open land, to rub against arching trees,
to wallow in luxurious mud so it cakes across my bulk.

And leave me to dream, alone, of breeding one calf at a time
while three-year olds jostle in the herd's warmth. We were clear
– towering dung marks our land. So be careful where you stand
for every one of your footsteps are taken in our footprints,
now footnotes to the Anthropocene epoch.

AFTER LENTINI

Giacomo da Lentini was a Sicilian poet who seems to have written the very

first sonnets. He was a notary at the the court of Frederick II in Palermo in the

early years of the 13th century. Sicily in that period was already multicultural

with scholars, philosophers, scientists and artists from the Christian, Judaic and

Muslim traditions sharing thoughts and insights. Giacomo absorbs and reworks

the Occitan traditions and poetic forms of southern France into local modes and

procedures. Interestingly there is no trace of his original Sicilian texts. We have

only the transcriptions into Tuscan. So translation and adjustment, not to mention

gentrification, in one way or another, is there in his poetry from the start.

RE:LODE 26

as you rummage

for recalcitrant *vongole*

in a brimming bowl

the muffled underwater

clicks & chatter

of the clams

add fresh percussive

highlights & deflections

to the deeper musics

of the valley

& the kitchen

where a lean trio

of anchovies

& four fat cloves

of this year's garlic

embark upon

a new collaboration

in the wide expanses

of your aluminium pan

whereas in itchy dreams

concocted by mosquitoes

& streams of vermentino

I saw you stick

a mini octopus

on the front

of your SG

which served as

temporary amp

& living strumbuddy

but also sang along

in wordless gurgling croons

such coy & plaintive tunes

as could be captured

by the engineers

at ECM

then blended with

the tread & lustre

of a battered old

acoustic bass

in timeless

Lombard airs

WOODSTOCK
after Jitish Kallat

Tomorrow I'm going back to Yasgur's farm:

smoking grass, music flattening trees,

whale-sound, cinnamon candles

and a kohl-eyed girl in a purple kaftan,

flowered peace-band circling long hair.

Cross-legged she sits among beautiful people

half a million strong.

Did they all become accountants?

I turn pages and pages of the battered journal,

even my writing has changed. Last week

at the Biennale, I stood in a doorway, in words

projected onto mist: *Become who you are,*

but just as songs rocked a town, I contain multitudes.

Tomorrow we're off to find one we left behind.

ROLE CHANGE

your hand is miniature in mine.
i run my finger over the wrinkled skin

of your body, afraid
to hold you, a quarter my genes,

your eyes shut fast like a puppy
exhausted after a long journey.

they point out a tiny black tear
falling from your pupil, but

it may help you see through dark times.
swaddled in cream, you wriggle and stretch,

supple as a yogi, then snuggle close.
i adjust the wrap. my lips brush your down,

feel the pulse of life in your fontanelle.
my fingers like sandpaper as i prise

open your fist. i want to find strong lines
of life, love and fate –

i know they're there.
but you wrap your fingers around mine,

hide your palm, clutch me tight.
so tight, i can lift you, dangling.

REBEL GUIDE

it's full-moon again time. before i die
i'll have seen one thousand. should i count

life in moons. call myself blood. call myself wolf.
call myself blue. years won't make me revered.

yet she is never witch-mooned. crone-mooned.
not decried as unstable when she is

edging away at the speed fingernails grow.
she's not in second childhood. third age.

as if it's an illness to reach three score and ten.
'dear'. drugged. dumpy sofa. a tree to be felled.

if old people are 'othered' does it make us
a different species. hearts have green energy.

last night i was picking oranges. this is a dream
of tears and anxiety. i've reached the waiting room

filled with the half-alive. threshold to a terrain
all fear to enter yet as rich with possibility

as the challenger deep. the elders' luminous
adventure. if we use all our eyes like stargazers.

I.

Likely harbour, you passed Sudan wearing a
life vest, or it could have been a palmed beach
towel. Where touts were a wild blessing I
found you rough as a flannel. Hidden, hoping
to unfold with humble logic. The bar steward
is intimating he's hungry. As you pull the
string on your vest, or slip off your bottoms
under the towel, you have a flush of sand
feeling palatable in the shish bicep gristle I
thought was guinea fowl. What's gathering
here is a gifted needlepoint defacement
where all the saints have arrows sticking out
the judgemental parts of their bodies. Your
bottoms are now covered in sand that is more
parts water than sand. The sunlight could still
learn to speak, spell aloud, break even having
to sneeze makes my words come thus: I do not
even think about it, which you say is pollen.
For the past six months perfect record inside
where it clots take the vaccine to Dagenham.
Cross jockeys will always play lift music, or
something like three children shifting to a
Greek Zorba. Fine, it starts slow, the first child
with a horde of iron filings she's using to fix
a cavity, then twenty years later the second
child approaches the patriarch of the Zorba
and says, 'I want to be vixen.' The patriarch
cracks a carbonated drink, the child now an
ill-tempered woman from the 1570s, as the
dance reaches its late stages, or what appears
as a vast and swirling polygonal shape formed
by linked hands which we came to call a circle
– had the belief been in the first place a burst

of colour before your eyes ascribed to swoon
of drunkenness – in which the third child, C
– through no fault of her own – has become
the Zorba's patriarch, giving away left right
abandon to the changing velocity of dance,
pissing himself in the process, he wishes for
a safe blockade where he can wait out the
rest of increasing speed, and in the end a dog
to finish what's fatigued on the floor. More
curious the storm rings out like money against
the windows' exterior, and I feel scared guano
of cave-dwelling bats who are also at the car
wash, and I am twelve, and the brushes and
the high-pressure rinse arch are coming to get
all of me, rinse me for what worth, and I am
gone scared as a spinning brush until someone
tells me what I have won. And didn't we wish
to eat forget laid waste to youth, and instead
this violence wears a fez that is not his to wear
it lift it releasing hornets. We talked it over,
impossible to stay, how could we afford to feed
the lamb and charge our phones overnight
and maintain a careful life and work balance.
A meaning beyond breath, inescapable as a
light filament popping what seemed right.
Taking on board more natural fats. The
iron filings will not cement as an impression.
A ding in the bone. We practised in church
between the pews, having been fragments for
a composition that has relevance to your life,
an aria gushed forth from between the gaps in
the staircase opening onto new pay channels
widening to levity compressed now to
industrious bead the potential fed to chickens

in the form of a pellet. O that expenditure or outflow or detox of feeling the next day brings with it trust in how the form and structure of rest must work, as they keep producing pellets, and a larger and more ecstatic production line to enforce them. Your wrist for interest. And your pay gap gallery, sunflower seeds shot over anyone who needs the distraction, shot through with rings of ash vitiligo stars are made of this.

【あぶさるど】

転覆、逆上、生命の捩じれ
度外れた哄笑、娼婦の白血球
駱駝の鈍感……豹の電流を注射しろ
バットの吸殻を拾う……ボロボロボ
赤練ガを焼いて■■■■におつっけろ
呼吸器械の喘ぎ……開かれた■
三百代言の首を■■■!!
狂人の真っ蒼に爛れた舌
麻痺した神経を硫酸で焼き尽せ
■■した犬の苦笑
接点は接点だ……
無限に楕円を描け、無限に転回しろ
生命の浪費は涎を垂らしている
ポコ　ポコ　ポコ　ポコ
凹凸　凸凹　凸ボコ　ボコ
ピストンの欠伸に触れるな
ブリキ板の方がお前の胸より柔らかい
血が青白く流れて、滴っている
ポタリ　ポタリ……タリ　タリ……
月が赤く笑っている
狂犬の死体を咬るスタカト
梟の眼は黒曜石よりも素晴らしい
逆さにつるされた胴体
風の残酷なフリュウトがきこえてきた
闇……大きなうつろな穴

1924

ABSOLUTE

Overthrow; unrest; existential parody;

obnoxious, inappropriate guffawing; slut leukocytes;

camel dumb head—*electric panther injection,*

scavenging for butts on the seafloor—worn,

      torn

      rumblings. Burn

the lacquered red atman sketches—

      songs of moths, congratulatory

      ditties—package

and mail the ashes to ____. Wheezing

of mechanical respirators, ligatured, spread-

      eagled on _____ racks.

___ the conmen's heads!—their tongues: festering,

      inflamed

      lunatic blue: acidize their palsied

      nerves—*dogs*, who ____, and fake

grin-stuck candor.

Tangent point is *the tangent point.*

Carve the ellipse on the infinity canvas,

(rotate). *Then, rotate again.*

("*Life of a Wastrel*," summed at his toes in a lake of drool.)

Ess   Ess   Ess   Ess
Craterous   Coarseness   Coarse-ness   Ness

PISTONS YAWNING, *don't touch!*—

        tin sheets softer than teats, bluish-white blood
flowing from tips—slowing to
     a drip,
dripping dripping ping ping

RED MOON, grinning (staccato): *gnawing on*

      rabies warm dog-corpses.

Eyes of OWL—more

      magnificent
      than obsidian—cold

bodies hung by purpled
ankles—fluyts

aired by brutish winds—

darkness......*a gaping.*

1924

August

THE DUST OF GREEN INFINITY CALLIPERS

A voluptuous nightingale of rum

solar osmosis causing moon pressure

spleens of yellowed tar morph to darkened camphor

enjambment embracing me with the dust of green infinity

calipers

your being an arc of ghostly cunning

being scores & scores of manipulated edens

being demonic crosses ingrained in your complication via a darkened valley of

diamonds not unlike an eel that swims through an arch of sound like a Cassowary magnet

burning like a golden sun under water

being a dietetic aurum

being cobalt samsaras tied to inky eyelid astonishment

INVISIBLE SAURIAN BALLET

A throat of quaking obsidian rivulets being blinded Salamander optics
that issue as wind from its sight less brush fire canals
from the depths of his sightless Ouroboric Stellar antimonies
into the outward darkness of non-existent retinal spinning

an optics of greenish aerial reverses being a heraldic dust storm
as eclipse being highly veiled opaline registration

being of higher interior transparency springing from higher rain demon bonnets
being a sigil condoned as porcelain Lion harassment

this saurian
christened as surgical invisibility
as sudden hydrogen glass coloured via the tone of an amber loins' mane while
drifting entering the central thickets of the Sun
thus
heating its fiery waterfall saliva
being spiders spun into curious astral magma
thus
its alter egos suspension
going out like a flare
its twisted shape
none other than obsession
none other than obsessional rhodopsin ballet

GERMINATION IN POST-OMEGA

Why not embody impermanence...
Huinening
— Sixth Patriarch in Zen . Buddhism

To persist as flask, as nocturnal monoron, completely unadorned by distant sets of judgment, a wayward nautical elixir, probing simultaneous zones refracted and spun beyond gregarious and spilled topologies and beacons, beyond each known inference of carved delusional facts and grammes, for instance, blankness as it exists beyond the ampersand, non symbolic of the turbulence engendered in profound and absolute extinction, but as an emptied and invincible volition without the terminology of transition, or propulsion without bleak electrum in its forays, there exists neutral thirst of momentum subsumed above the balanced ray of opposition, the lightness solar coast with its minerals in diffusion with its itinerant prosthesis by compound within its dormant alchemical emission, this is the internal carrier, the swimmer across Suns as alien myomycetes as orbits throughout various Stellar condensation, say, the shape of miraculous Hellebores tuned by a-demonstrative pulsation, by realms that link carbon with scarred and torrential magnets of heat, with raw creative transference, the spore by its nature amidst the yellowed heart of suspension, amidst caliginous soporific engulfment, amidst hidden and toppled pyres in various proto degrees across prolific colouration of neutrality, of various guiles of potentia, above the apex of signals, the spore consumed by ironic, by vibrational wavering being fecund storms between dimensions in which a cloud of selenium or cobalt, or the unprecedented tungsten elemental, as in the phase of protracted nuclear electrics as with scandium, or beryllium, so that the sum of its distances from any fixed or general point is non-specific, is the factor where geometry absconds its merciless eloquence with photometry of mirrors as shattered elongation, of disembodied emulsion, being rudiment, taking on sulfurous candescence as liberating haze,conflicts ceasing to evolve from any populous matter, from any seeded fixation, as if, all dimensional conflicts were broken and left inchoate beyond in-fixed eternity, as anti-mesmerization, as to one single bearing, or tendency that occludes adventitious graces, that flow via inordinate meta-kinetic, alive with beatific occultation, as to the anti-sired, as to hollowed nursing evanescence, not Hesperian or auroral, the latter being the flight of the spore, symbolized as trans-galactic simoom, beyond the dice of craft, beyond motion as counted fate, there persists convergence, not only as extinguished hermeneutics, but as the selfless void of Ravines...

СЪРЦЕТО НЕ Е СЪЗДАТЕЛ

Помпената станция на радостта –
в края на пътеката.
Страхът, че ако поискам да те вдигна,
ще залитна и с облекчение ще изсипя товара си по склона.
Радостта, че живото тяло тежи повече от мъртвото,
защото се движи –
както вятърът прави студа
по-силен.
Страхът, че ще се изпънеш като струна
или панически ще потърсиш с крака дъното
като плувец, който не вярва в Бог
или който в този момент е забравил,
че вярва.
Страхът, че веднъж съблечени,
ще ни е страх да признаем колко ни е студено,
и радостта, че и другият се страхува.
Ще привличаме мълниите?
Мокрият
не се страхува от поръсване
със здравец.

Кръвта изкачва своите върхове.
Сърцето изпраща и приема пътници,
повдига
и те прави птица –
с мокри пера, с вода в мотора, със сухо гърло –
но птица.
И все пак сърцето не е създател.

THE HEART IS NOT A CREATOR

The pumping station of joy –
at the end of the path.
The fear that if I want to lift you
I will lurch and dump my load on the slope with relief.
The joy that a living body weighs more than a dead one
because it moves –
as wind makes cold
stronger.
The fear that you will stretch like a string
or anxiously search for the bottom with your feet
like a swimmer who doesn't believe in God
or has momentarily forgotten
he believes.
The fear that, once undressed,
we will be afraid to admit how cold we are,
and the joy that the other is also afraid.
Will we attract strikes of lightning?
The wet one
is not afraid to be sprinkled
with geranium leaves.

Blood climbs its peaks.
The heart sends and receives passengers,
lifts up
and makes you a bird –
with wet feathers, water in the engine, a dry throat,
but a bird.
And yet the heart is not a creator.

СЪРЦЕТО НЕ Е СЪЗДАТЕЛ

Спомняш ли си как започнах да духам в ухото ти? Трябваше да наподобя различни ветрове. Нощен бриз, който духа от сушата към водата и е перфектен за тихо тръгване, ураганен горещ казахстански ибе, който обстрелва с дребни камъчета барабаните на полето, сух харматан, който оцветява Атлантика с кръвта на Сахара, арабски самум, който смесва желязото на земята с мехурчетата на морето, италиански суховей сироко, който с горещината си предизвиква безумие и убийства от загуба на посоката, пролетен мистрал, който насича на филийки марсилските изгреви, синайски шарав, който изпива водата от очите, студено уругвайско памперо с много дъжд, който те обвива като шал, хартумски хабуб, който закрива с прах всичко и те кара да се чувстваш зазидан във въздуха, шквал, който рязко преобръща солидни лодки, леден трамонтана, спускащ се отгоре като паднал ангел. Страшни, нежни, меки като сюнгер и твърди като бетон. Постигнах само смях.

THE HEART IS NOT A CREATOR

Do you remember how I started blowing in your ear? I had to imitate various winds. A night breeze, which blows from land to water and is perfect for quietly setting out; a hurricane hot Kazakh ibe, which pounds the drums of the field with little stones; a dry harmattan, which colours the Atlantic with the blood of the Sahara; an Arabian simoom, which mixes the iron of the earth with the bubbles of the sea; an Italian dry sirocco, which with its heat causes madness and murder from a loss of direction; a spring mistral, which cuts Marseille sunrises into slices; a Sinai sharab, which absorbs the water from your eyes; a cold Uruguayan pampero with lots of rain, which wraps you like a shawl; a Khartoum haboob, which covers everything in dust and makes you feel immured in the air; a squall, which violently overturns solid boats; an icy Tramontane descending from above like a fallen angel. Scary, tender, soft as a sponge and hard as concrete. All I got was a laugh.

AFFORDABLE THERAPY

when she died, I cried as if I knew her
& every time after in my floods of tears
I blamed it on my dead aunt
till at some point my mum intervened—
my brother does the same, but he blames the dog.
the vulnerable bit is already happening,
I am crying to a stranger again. In adulthood,
all my embarrassment became second-hand
as I detached from myself & checked in & out
of relationships till I found I was a common
denominator (maths was never a strong suit)
in my inner child work, my nervous system,
recalibrated like a DS with a chewed stylus
probably still in my blood metaphorically,
or accumulated in microplastics along with
the chewing gum blown in a permanent bubble
as to make a permanent gap—
Is this the best place to start?
I took the advice & ran with it putting obstacles
between myself & the feeling a CAHMS cup of tea
a shower a long walk down a wet beach
but shame swells up swole & soon enough
I have forgotten which timeline I am in—
the feeling started when   no, it all started
when   no, there was no beginning there was just—
no, let me start again, please can we begin again?
my feelings became big & gross & hard to conceptualise
so, to save on the brainpower,
I decided I am the first person to ever feel shame,
or at least it feels that way—
next to a photo of myself, I have captioned
'I feel sorry for her, but not me,' I can't quite explain why—

I can't let myself down like this, I want to exist to myself,

I am trying to tell you all of this,

that the shame grows in the damp silence, the pause,

the parenthesis (where the gaps between the words

say the things I had hoped were not possible)

KNOW THYSELF

if antibody levels can be tracked by monitoring
then I can transgress past the need to know anything
let my blood become the sum of my experience
& chalk these symptoms down to *who-knows-what*

I watch my dinner spit & boil over,
spinning in the soft glow of the microwave
imagining driving myself in for an M.O.T.
& letting a strong man do the heavy lifting
reducing my mood to a smiley face on a post-it
or tapping my head like fixing a TV antenna

I feel most alive when the disqualified realm
of what we don't know becomes insurmountable
when I look into the world   & it looks back
when the comedic timing collapses
& I catch the microwave:
00:01

WHAT IS OURS

Within those flowing hills and rugged coast
communities cement themselves into history:
reigning champions of child poverty and suicide.
For the hills and coast stretch far beyond the line
where the House begins to care;
their bloodlines cared, they might remember,
for by this coast and in these hills
they built their industries,
and in those industries, our bloodlines worked,
choked and died before fifty. Mined, built, crafted ships
with their bare hands and formed connections with the world,
for an Empire to plunder and pillage and call it protection.
But in our hills and by our coast,
character blooms infinitely.

NORTH SEA FROM A DISTANCE

Birdsong mounts damp from the Mouth –
odd to feel its warmth. Lilac breaks the day
beyond the warehouse, swallows the shooting
range with pre-dawn beads a haze in their wake.
The beeps and rumbles and podcast voices roll
between the ears as we meet morning, and we fear
for a second, uniforms fighting through the lilac
and the haze, crossing the road of broken workers
in their broken cars and gunning us down.

Our bones to rest by those charred in blackdamp
pockets, the insulation between coal walls.
Smog-stained and littered with ashen scars above
each serpentine divide, sea clouds perspire salt spray
to scrub soot and reduce the clank of tools and crush
of earth underfoot.

the distant mark of a timeless civilisation
appropriated by those already forgotten
trapped between colours
reduced to sepia
a jutting outcrop of navy blooms
On the border between factory and field
green and grey
red a generation ago
thick with blood that pulsed
now blue

severed.

SCUM

Judge Holden and three
Jacks to be cut
usurped the order to proclamations
of history — it's how it's always been.
Ivory knives scalped the vests
of the largest plague pit, dusted
them down and pumped shit into their systems —
SCUM TAX scratched on the invoice.
Generation [insert] should see compensation.
For now, the notice is a measure too extreme,
industrial action a beacon for tabloid torture —
bastard wasps to something sweet.
The Derruti t-shirt and Goldman quotes are packed
away come Monday — I'm not afraid of ruins
but unemployment is something different.
Low-emission zones are nice,
but so are mandatory Eco-funerals
for the billionaires,
enforced by stripped fossil fuel
licenses and arse-slapping taxes.

I'm sorry, Sir. If you don't have an Eco-service, we'll be forced to sink your yacht.

But I'm not dead yet.

I'm sorry, Sir, that's not my fucking problem.

EQUINOXE

March arrives

The snowdrops have company in the verges

And lone pheasants' fields are overrun with songbirds,

Spindle-boned and sinewy boys

Brush off leaf litter

Lichen

Root and sycamore seed

The mole burrows shallow

The footsteps form on hardened mud

And the Winter Wizard must leave

He comes for his doll,

His boy,

His bobbin,

And I kiss you once more

Return my soul to this realm

And the magic leaves me.

His hands are gnarled and ashen,

His snowdrops have wilted

His beard is full of bones,

Tiny,

delicate,

Sharp

He will return,

Beard, Bobbin and conical hat

But for now,

It is spring,

And the willow calls me,

Not dying,

But radiant.

BOBBIN LOST

When the Wizard was young,

And full of ideas,

He built a small village

Based on Bognor Regis.

He built a viaduct for ants

A carousel for lice

He captured the rodents,

Made horses of mice.

His Knitting Doll was king, up high in the priory

He oversaw rain, sleet and snow

Without comment or irony.

When the Knitting Doll was lost,

The Wizard grew mad,

Burst the banks of the viaduct,

Squashed lice beneath hand.

The knitting Doll knew

The knitting Doll fled

Threw himself to the river,

Left love for dead.

DO YOU REMEMBER WHEN I TRIED TO BE GOOD
after Ocean Vuong

I wore a dress to my aunt's sixtieth birthday party.

It was a bad time.

I wasn't the right person for him.

How could anyone want to live again.

One day the sun will stop burning & I won't

be there to help other people & everything

alive makes me grieve. A fool, I still go to therapy

just to confirm that I care.

It was too dark & I left the house with my dead phone.

I still think about my pet goldfish buried

in Golden Syrup tins. Meaningful things

won't always be happy things.

I came out to my Reverand by email & felt like praying.

On the coach to Yosemite, I watched two people

like me hold hands. I tried to make eye contact

but it was like trying to control a dream

when you're just about to wake up.

I have a drawer in my room just for stones.

My dad is worried that his uncle was a Nazi.

I kept a notebook as a teenager for important information.

Genocides. I know how they happen.

People will do anything to be good.

I fell through ice & breathed in smoke to keep warm

but we don't talk about that.

HOPPER'S GAZE

like most things important it took longer to realise

than it should have but looking at Edward Hopper's

paintings of women in rooms before COVID-19

makes me angry at his simplified version of women

reinforcing our sexist roles in the home staring out

of windows instead of painting them

like the men who dominate the art galleries

Room in New York depicts a woman in a dress

sitting on a piano stool in a way which would make

composing her own piece of music impossible

whilst the man in the picture

reads the newspaper in his waistcoat and tie

an outfit which maybe the woman wanted to wear

whilst she danced in one of the few dyke bars

but instead wakes up frustrated and alone

like the woman in *Morning Sun* with her husband

out of the picture and sleeping with whoever

he wants since he controls their finances so she

gazes out of the window her only comfort

the colour blue and an empty bed

24 HOUR TESCO

it's too late to remember what I came to Tesco for

but I know it had something to do with the last time we spoke

in your room we were both in facemasks and I was thirsty

which made me tell you the truth for once admitting

that I needed a glass of water more than anything else

to carry on you found a glass you were protecting in a drawer

from COVID-19 and walked out of the door for the first time

leaving me alone in the room

like life beyond therapy where you'll leave the world before me

now in Tesco I walk towards the boxes of tissues and think about

whether you've ever had a client who has walked away

with your tissue box before or asked you where you bought

them from so they could have a souvenir with which to say goodbye

September

A few months after his birth I experienced a period of occasional hallucinations. I never really admitted them as such, even to the NHS therapist whose chair being higher than mine made me feel pleasantly/uncomfortably like a child. I declared them as *not hallucinations exactly*, but they were and she echoed them back to me without my reserve—a product of not wanting to seem *dramatic* and also a fear of the powerlessness that comes with being deemed mad. I think of author Janet Frame's near-miss with a lobotomy, and all the millions of others not saved by their own poetry.

My hands, holding my baby, were not my own, that was the hallucination. It wasn't that they felt like someone else's, but that they looked like hers. Not similar or reminiscent, but as if they were hers. It struck me with the feel of a possession or a haunting. And I am reminded, in a fashion of odd circular connectedness, of the haunting in Frame's novel *The Carpathians*—such a beautifully rendered ghostly presence, a hallucination perhaps.

I remembered, too late to share it with the tired but always engaged therapist, a moment shortly after my grandmother's death. My grandfather took my hands and told me they were like hers (a different her)—it was stifling. I'm fairly sure they are nothing like hers were, we were physically dissimilar. Perhaps he was hallucinating them, projecting them. They had spent decades in almost exclusively each other's company and were very much in love.

I liked her, this first therapist—a little odd, very present—but when she said *why should he be different?* not really as a question, I knew it was another wall. Did I answer, *why shouldn't he be?* I should have.

Perhaps it is just the effect of the well-documented sleep-deprivation that so often accompanies early parenthood, or perhaps the neurological changes that pregnancy, birth and breastfeeding bring about, but I feel more vulnerable to ghosts—mine and others'. Or perhaps I am unhinged by the terrifying normalness of this creature-person who is suddenly with me always and whose near-silent sleep I have disturbed without fail for a full 365 days, in an effort to detect his breath. *Happy birthday my darling.* The rise and fall of his ribs is so slight that to feel it I must hold my own breath while my hand rests there. Yet his existence is so powerful, and his absence so unimaginable (or sickeningly possible), I have written him in to memories from before.

A rose garden in Ohio, all bare black and winter cropped, in a blizzard. I was alone and, I seem to remember, feeling especially alone and a little desperate. But, overlaid, like a transparency, I remember my pregnant self there, a self that wouldn't come to be for more than a year, and never in Ohio.

DAVID LYNCH IN GLASGOW

Stepping out of the cinema onto wet tarmac, I am flanked by quiet tenements and glowing fog.

A seedy low-rise hotel on Argyll Street looks invitingly warm against the night.

The few lights illuminate perspiration-drenched windows, shapes of figures in the steam.

Beyond the hotel, the Clyde is black, no one around but the uniformity of trees at equidistant intervals in beds of white concrete, like rows of cactus plants in a suburban LA home.

Through the corrugated iron industrial estate, Nicholas Cage sings absurdly in my ears.

A brown envelope containing a VHS tape greets me at my doorstep, I swear I will never watch it, but one day I will.

WHO AM I?
A cento of Bob's letters

I am for once not sauna-bound

I go to roller discos and play the violin

I feel very lucky and weirdly undeserving

I'd say a good third of my day is spent fobbing people off

Sometimes I feel like I'm just living out this tired, homosexual cliche

repeated on a loop, just with different music and different medication

I go on Instagram and look at the drag cycles of Kent

in my brown lederhosen

I don't think I convinced anyone that I was into leather

I'm listening to Tchaikovsky's violin concerto

which makes everything sound more dramatic than it actually is

It took me hours to hacksaw my way through a kitchen knife

I've got very good at disassociating

I guess this is what a lifetime of precarity does to the psyche

we shouldn't beat ourselves up

I don't think we could have moved further away from each other

One day I'll set up a sex club and it'll be like the set of Fun House

I'm slowly beginning to trust the sense of home

I MAKE PEOPLE INTO MY DAD

When I let some fucking asshole have me I just go with whatever he wants

I'm bad when I don't know what people want, I always make the wrong decision

I thought I was a total prick for not just giving you what you wanted

I'm telling you I can't be saved

I can say for sure I have a cute ass

I've jacked off thinking about you holding me in your arms

I don't want to talk about the details anymore

TANGERINE

A tangerine in a pigeon-hole. Left by your ghost? I go through the motions in my baggy dress, mascara and lip-gloss. Do I pass as a good employee? I have taken the tough fruit of grief. I crumble into a crumpled tissue in the toilet cubicle at lunch. Peel the skin of rotten citrus back. My soul has sepsis. Council tax to pay.

IMPOSSIBLE STORY

The mouth cannot lose the tongue,

but it can be silenced by fear.

Chewing on toffees.

Censoring verbs.

Writing an impossible story.

I cannot create from clay

when the creation is stuffed

into a dark cupboard.

I go out to capture a flash of sun,

it is raining cats and rats.

I touch my crocodile skin,

starved of nutrients and care.

They say, *the Holy Spirit lives within.*

I try to keep my heartrate down

to make it a comfortable home.

Storm-licked in our apartments.

We should all take to the streets.

MONDAY

Every Monday she wears lace gloves.

Every Monday she hides the white buds of teeth

when she asks me for rent, rent, rent, rent, rent, rent, rent, rent, rent, rent, rent, rent, rent, rent, rent rent, rent, rent, rent, rent, rent, rent, rent, rent, rent, rent, rent, rent, rent, rent, rent, rent, rent, rent rent, rent, rent, rent, rent, rent, rent, rent, rent, rent, rent, rent, rent, rent, rent, rent, rent, rent, rent.

No slither of emotion.

Every Monday, her eyes: white as eggs.

Every Monday it is crisis o'clock.

READING THE MARKERS OF AUTISM IN GIRLS, I BECOME ⩔

a nun picking roses ⩔ her hands are many small stigmata ⩔ that is the feeling of outside on her skin ⩔ wrapping her head in fabric makes her feel closer to god ⩔ in this version of things god is becoming overwhelmed by her own experience of herself ⩔ her manifestations ⩔ when sunset is pooling down glistening ⩔ rose struck ⩔ the sky is the colour of her old school uniform ⩔ she understands suddenly why it was always so hard ⩔ noisy ⩔ the safety of the stone nunnery of silence ⩔ of not being god getting overwhelmed by the noises of the bus ⩔ the beautiful babies screaming being a tiny drop of water bending ⩔ reflecting endlessly ⩔ maybe she has found the reason why she was able to create something so huge so overwhelming something moving in so many directions of red perfect symmetry then suddenly blood

LOVER / PRIORY

priory

o disciples! circling

glasses like singing angels

tender doubles pouring wine

tracing earth with their feet, eating flesh

open like a squat   what wounds!

i feel like an animal   worse

an animal i dont know, drunken

were they punishing   us /

i feel like unpaid for space   so

many ruined objects! even the rooms

are empty   disciples! like insects

each footstep is monk on their knees

priory,,   your body is what

they are prizing,   palms

weaving desire, close fingers

pocked with prayer

& drops of deep red in the cracks

& wanting,,

lover

i feel closer

to you, touching your feet

hard skin like comfort

thumb to arch   walking the priory

of course i find you, that is my

orientation, in terms of attachment

the monks are attached to god

the priory is attached to the ground

                              pacing our desires by the stone

                              each footstep, we are here

                              surrounded by brambles

                              drinking wine & touching

                              things gently

BARBENHEIMER

Imagine clouds at sunset —

orange, hot fuchsia —

a powder rounded with fire.

Directions in pink: *alarmed,*

press here, radiant.

Smiles painted on surfaces,

her core charged on conveyor

belts of want, waiting

for girls' arms' reach to expand.

'You're a bomb, Barbie.' ('Thanks, Ken!')

'Boom, boom, so much fun.

Let's fill your tank, light you up.'

Curves perfect, atomic; waist

un-elastic. Step

forward, soles arching in air.

HITCHCOCK'S VERTIGO

There she died, where redwood trees took no notice:

her hair spreads strays of blonde in Fort Point Bay.

They drive to her suicide scenes and kiss,

her dress sinking downstream with the bouquet.

Did you have dreams, Madeleine, of what his

shipyard would mean before you scaled the stairway?

Her shadow slips into his hug, an abyss

of deadly leaps that scratch noon's backlit runway.

San Francisco waves pull away what's amiss

in her life. That wasn't part of the play.

                        Her heels ascend in shadows, the stairs' spiral.

                               Johnny-O, Johnny-O. Will you go on?

                            Inside a hospital, he visits final

                cuts of her soaked blonde hair, a rope to atone.

                            'Pain is only palpable, not arrival',

                  they explain and add that when he is alone

seeing ladders turns his mind centrifugal.

Fold away maps, they won't show where I've gone;

I gathered dahlias, a sense of normal.

His mind lowers in shadows. The stairs spiral.

1.   Mimo has work to do, the worst work: checking

live feed that doesn't nourish him

from facial recognition software tied to cameras

around the country. He checks

that the software is working – verifies

tags in Mall CCTV, security in nightclubs,

faces framed for scrutiny. It was from the point

that the voice of his Director began bleeding

into his own inner voice that he found himself

finding the prospect of windows and of memories

irresistible. He needs to get things clear

or get well clear of them – through glass

and plexiglas he sees things differently.

When he moves up to the window and eyes

out, however muffled and uncommon the state he is in,

it is clear where the feelings should be: down there

on the street, sandwiched between other glass panes.

He's watching the arm move

in a shop, stress and compression and stretch,

it rakes what is drifting away (robot blood, fine river sand).

A second arm takes a bottle. With glass you can get away

with a lot of things; but airplane pilots whose eyes

are damaged by plexiglas shards

fare better than those injured by standard glass –

better compatibility between plexiglas and human tissue.

Mimo is intensely interested in how he will look,

in what he will keep.

Your nose is too close to the screen.

There's the Director again, voicing:

A face at a window

for no apparent reason should have a thumb

in its mouth. Or, if the face is not childish it is free-

floating, blotted white by the darkness of the room.

Rub out the formal relations, look through the glass

at the slides we prepared, be ready for chapters

to come in the form of spacing out.

                    Mimo keeps watching

the arm get confused about the room it is in.

        Loss of your own making.

                    In the majority of applications

plexiglas will not shatter but break

into large dull pieces. Squint through it, glance at it;

what matter? what kind of keep?

what hold? It looked like a sack,

or maybe a deformed animal,

visible behind the middle column, mostly to the right.

It expanded and contracted, pulsing

like some kind of smear.

2.   Loss of your own making. Mimo takes it to heart,

wants so to get it clear to get clear of it, yet

when he tries to take things back he gets an image

of his first aquarium. A shell ricochets in the memory,

sounding his past and catching a stress point

in the screen. Floods of water, plastic forts, weeds and silver-

bellied fish slip and jump around him, pooling

in the room. Those two little round things,

the shape of a bumble-bee, flashing past and displaying

on their rear end a round eye bordered with blue,

are they really fish?

                He squeezes his mind firmly,

tries to bring it all back. He can remember

some parental face as it gaped down, remember

the lino, remember how in that moment the structure

of arms corresponds to the structure of legs.

He can put that box back, or he can kneel

to feel surging water. But the fish:

of the dull-coloured kind, or pastel grunts,

he nearly always sees several of the same family at once,

but of the brightly coloured within his field of vision

there is *one* blue and *one* black angel-fish.

Like the hardwood forests, and the songbirds

too, the idea that these fish could cease

while he is 'working', that those might be the last,

brings on an attack of nausea, and he screens

his eyes against them.

            I will rip the souped-up spine I added

        to your ribs back out of your back before I let you flow away as the loss

of your own making.

When Mimo makes a spectacle of himself

he's learned he needs to pool a little dance and try to keep it

to himself. An aquarium is good measure of a spine's hardness;

ideally they are compatible, descending together towards soft

flesh and its opening: no one ever shattered an ass

to fragments; no one threatens to actually steal your anus.

But it can slip away from you while nobody is watching.

That parental face...

That parental face impresses him

transparency is the best form of detachment:

look me in the face and tell me how you love, loop back

past the one blue and the one black angel-fish to where the crack

began.

He wants a vacation, can't stop looking away.

Designers started building much bigger aquariums when Plexiglas

could be used, but it's been avoided for other large-scale constructions

since the Summerland disaster. Then there's the hardest love

that will never abolish the distance between one window

and another, plus pressure of being already squeezed

between those panes – *Tell me!* – a new slide

every time you try to think – *How you love!*

To make plexiglas you pour polymerized

methyl methacrylate between two glass panels that are enclosed

by flexible sidebands. During the polymerization process

in a water quench the material shrinks slightly and the glass

plates are drawn towards one another. The finished Plexiglas®

sheet can easily be removed from the glass plates.

'Easy!?', thinks Mimo, needing a break, feeling the screens

and the surfaces form. Nothing novel there.

October

HERE WHAT LICKS SINS

I'm sorry we're moving, I'm sorry we're moving again. Our last stop will be your hometown. The one with all of the hauntings. This is how the world ends. A ghost is never what you think, you can't catch a ghost like you catch a butterfly. A storm of empty crows perches on the telephone lines in August, and someone you know will die and they'll die by a bullet, a knife, an explosion or a long string of cigarettes. They'll die of a bad dream of a long winter. They'll die by their own hand. The way I die is by breaking my back while trying to make a window where there isn't one. It looked easy and took less than a minute. We don't talk about these things, the ways we can make it all go away. You can't kill a ghost, but if you could wouldn't you be tempted to try? There's too much noise, too much static in my head. When we're done, we'll sit out the silence in the woods with you. We'll be quiet and patient with ourselves as we watch this world burn.

THE WINE OF SIN IS HERE

Sorry, we're moving, sorry, we're moving again. Our last stop is a town like yours. The only people who dream about how the world will end are never who you think. You can't dream like a butterfly. In August, void clouds will buzz over the phone lines and someone you know will be shot, stabbed, blown up or killed by a long chain of cigarettes. They die from bad sleep & long winters. They die by their own hands, to break my back and create a window where there is none. It's easy and takes less than a minute. We are not talking about them, but about ways to remove them. You can't kill a ghost, but if you could, wouldn't you be tempted to try? I have a lot of noise in my head all the time. When we are done, we will sit quietly with you in the forest. While this world burns we will remain calm and patient.

HERE IS THE WINE OF SIN

Sorry, I'm moving, sorry, I'm moving again. Our final destination is a town like yours. You would think that people are the only ones who dream about the end of the world, but animals do too. You can't dream like a butterfly. In August, a blank cloud will appear over the phone line and someone you know will be shot, stabbed, blown up, and killed with a cigarette. They'll die from lack of sleep or a long winter. They will die from cutting back and creating a windowless space. It's not about them, it's about ways to get rid of them. You can't kill a ghost, but if you could, would you try? I have a constant noise in my head. When we are done, we will sit with you quietly in the forest. Let's be patient and calm while this all burns.

VAN GOGH'S LAST SELF-PORTRAIT

Picture: a crossword of makeup

an old Welsh poem on canvas of the past,

a mirror to the future

to remember the essence

of what I was.

Oh yes, I got days of my madness

days of sun-scorched Provence

a fire on my skin, mornings' dew

tears on the cherry tree's cheek

that stretches out its fragile fists towards the azure,

the late sun

setting like a snail across the wheat fields,

and nights of indigo

and the wretches of the city

whisper from each street.

I was a sorcerer of faces,

I was a wizard of images,

I was an artist.

And the whole thing comes back to this –

the magic that twinkles from the sky on an August night

in the round hollows of the pools of my eyes,

a rainbow of humanity that I saw

a lock in the casket of the skull

and the golden force

that shines from the background of yellow corn

so weak

as the gleanings of a ginger beard

that cling to my chin.

I'm broken in.

and in the fakery of days to come I will be so;

the fox that grew wise,

the flame that became established,

without a sign

for you that came from the woe I saw,

except for the pangs of paint in the background

that meander forever

towards – what?

HYDRANGEAS

The pink ultra-pink, the blue a calcification of blue

that scratches the afternoon like chalk on a blackboard of yesteryear

the way that they grow

in boiling hot gardens, a municipality in the sun.

Their toilet-paper colours.

The leaves, like palms fat in their width that say

"I've nursed roots by now".

Even the white ones – too white, somehow,

not the flimsy whiteness of Japanese paper

but the whiteness of a nothing-nothing, an absent whiteness,

negative, empty, too bloody-bloody boring.

A sign of being middle aged is liking hydrangeas,

discussing the way the soil will

colour some blue, the others pink,

conferring on how to fool nature

through shovelling lime on top of acidic soil.

Doting then on the way

each flower is a smaller flower, a star that nestles

inside a bigger star; perfect, round, worlds,

infatuated with their beauty in their decline,

a sober rainbow

the brown, the grey, the yellow, glorying in their hydrangeas.

BLANK VERSE SONNET ON HERE WE GO AGAIN

America I feel your guilty shrugging

The cotton sliding from your shoulder clos

-er to your throat I feel it   at my throat

America your dry   but not unpleasant

Cottony hands they're sliding from the right

And from the left they're sliding up my chest

From just above my heart and   yes from to

The right of it my heart   feels like a col

-lar tightening feels   like I'm feeling it

For you the iron collar of your shrug

And guilty   yes but guilty like a child

Licking the chocolate from his fingers after

The grocer told him not to steal   and turned

Back to his phone   and would not raise his head

TRUMP ALONE ON THE MORNING OF HIS SECOND INAUGURATION

You better fucking   shit you fucking better

Pardon those fucking assholes fucking   Fauci

Milley and fucking   Cheney you saw how she

Betrayed her country me you're   gonna let her

Just get away with it   you're an abettor

To it's the   greatest crime   it is   and now the

People won't ever get justice I mean wow the

Depths Joe you   piss on me and you'll get wetter

Than me you piss   on my inaugura-

tion you'll be crawling through the puddle on

Your knees to kiss my fucking knuckles   what

For what   for nothing   *I* have fucking mon-

ey not those pricks   enjoy your fucking   hut

Your dirt   enjoy being good Joe   how's the pay

ELIZABETHAN SONNET ON HE'S THINKING OF PHOTOSHOP BUT CAN'T REMEMBER THE NAME

I saw my blood and wondered   had I cut her

The woman in the picture agent in

The picture her   I don't remember what her

Name was I must have known it knew it when

Before she rushed the stage to what I guess

Take the next bullet   but I think the guy

Was dead already   how'd they hide the mess

His blood and insides from the pictures I

Was told they hid it   if I knew computers

I'd find the   pictures of the guy myself

I tell my guys   *I want to see the shooter's*

Body   they talk about my "mental health"

Somebody Elon   anybody show

Me how to hide the blood   and then I'll know

MOVEMENT

i.

The dead sun's necklace is what I remember

most, the conspiracy of hawthorn converging on Troost Avenue, the redbrick

songbook of a spiral mirror. Have you been caressed by your own food supply?

Have you descended the cane of the rose down into your navel? Did you bleed

enough? The wrecking ball slick with albumen destroys no matter

which way it turns for help, and the addicted father in the park screams

Swing batter, swing. It's hard to ignore crabapples when they have your name

written on them, when they have been airborne since 1897. I used to be home

-less, too. Every *hello* I entertained was preauthorized, and I would pitch

my hammock between two yews above the sidewalk. Hell turned out to be a breeze

-way between two heavens, but I settled for a crumb of angel food.

CODA

i.

This is the silver

cornflower blue I remember, the dog-day

cicadas hypnotized by their own plainsong

and the puppy star barking

from behind my uvula, mouth

filling with the black gold

Achilles' mother dipped him in

each morning, my own mother's white noise

machine protecting her sleep

from me, and how I woke at the southern

terminus of Rainbow Boulevard

ii.

the terminus of Rainbow Boulevard

gets lost in throats of country

clubs and the shallow, broken neck

of Brush Creek, traditional Latin

Mass harmonizing with the photon

beams of Westwood Radiology

at this nexus of wealth and malaise

crowned by tasteless stonecrop

older now and place-weary I realize

our sickness is a standard

in the Great American Songbook

THE VITALIST FINDS EMPLOYMENT IN A FUNERAL PARLOUR,

where, in a back room, she helps devise new merchandise: 'Ashes to Casserole Dishes', 'Departed Fistbumps', 'Relax Relics & Grief Salts for the Bath'—and other dead-friendly ventures. She fantasises about a 'Lock-it Locket' wearable key—which secures a door you never want to open again. Her bosses are impressed and though she works for a sub-living wage, without holiday or sick pay, there are posthumous perks, and a coffin thrown in. Also use of the garage as a gym when it is empty.

Treadmill of the dead.

THE VITALIST AND GEORGE ELIOT GO ON HOLIDAY TOGETHER

They wear lace caps. They chatter under the towering funnels and masts of the passenger steamships in the port jutting up into the low clouds of the grey day. George Eliot wants to circle the earth in search of successive autumns like a bird. The Vitalist envisages spring in Vienna. They tussle, mildly. Later George Eliot declares, heaving her black portmanteau onto a bunk bed in the cabin, that the highest—*most moral*—thing of all is *sweet abnegation, delicious self-denial*—and so they must live on holiday as if they'd never migrated. The Vitalist is beguiled by this idea of *non-life*, advocated with such clarity and enthusiasm, as well as by the nothingy pale sea which has started putting on a performance for the new passengers through the steamy porthole. She bags the top bunk. For the next 14 days, including 3 given over to mal de mer, she observes George Eliot rising shortly after 4am, rebuttoning her floor-length nightdress, exchanging a linen night cap for the winged-lace day cap and laying out a bank of gold-nibbed pens and sepia pages by the candlestick on the cabin desk. GE's face is all hollows and angles as she focuses. Her eyes lift occasionally to the cabin walls and she seems to scan fully peopled cities in the whorls of the honey-coloured timbers, then untold vistas in the undulations and desultory white horses of the dingy sea, always rearing up and climbing the eternal O of the porthole. The Vitalist meditates on the top bunk, sharpens pencils, chops candies and nuts, letting them down in a crocheted pouch to the lower bunk, along with occasional notes offering to do GE's laundry and making random observations. They breakfast on pastries some goodly period past their best, and raisins and half-oranges. After a fortnight they call at a port which the Vitalist does not catch the name of. GE has booked ahead at a pension run by three rosy landlady-philosophers, who take it in turns to speak, a third of a sentence each, bestowing verbs, nouns and particles equally and equably between their interlocutors. *Suffering ennobles the crudest creatures*, George proclaims, fretting for a pen. The Vitalist supplies a jotter, opened at a page hurriedly titled 'Tribulations'. They accept an attic room which looks out over red roofs and a crooked blue sky. The leaves on the trees show a definite twist of autumn. The Vitalist dreams of cherry blossom.

THE VITALIST WADES THROUGH A BOG OF MISOGYNY

a stinkhorned off-white mess like sour cream, hiding stinging fish and sink holes, a whole sucking morass between her and the next milestone, a whole smirking mire.

DESIRE FOR A FUTURE PORCH ON WHICH TO PLAY MY FUTURE BANJO

i've rarely held paradise but this will do fine; lacy insects

      impractical to the touch

and me, stepping through the mosquito net, looking at our rental

      dead in the eyes

which are your eyes by association... *amphibious green...*

      the whole palo verde...

and what did we expect ?? this is what happens when an architect

      and a landscape gardener

have sex for the first time; they climax in fleshy succulents,

      sticky hibiscus pinks,

an entire rustic porch !! ++ plus banjo ++ plus stool

architectural digest = desperate to broaden their audience.

      no this is not the poem

in which i imagine my air bnb host is starring in an

      interior design porno

but the garden is a setup. the setup is a sexy fire blazing

      all over the hills...

fuck whoever in the land of the free !! too much sun

      on the mountainside[1]

but fuck whoever !! if you fire your arrows into clay pots

      they'll photosynthesize and become the whole

homophobic tree for achilles' ghost to hate.

---

1. See *The Uneven Distribution of AI's Environmental Impacts* on Harvard Business Review by Shaolei Ren and Adam Wierman.

the birds were windchimes in another life — the windchimes

were running water

with the hollywood glitz left in. can you tell i am trying not

to be jaded

as i imagine the future? can you tell it's the same light on my

fingers so gold it peeled paint after paint

from off the front porch?

CAPER IN THE CASTRO[2]

Before Castro 'we weren't just in closets we were under rocks'
— D.Jones

if you ever woke up in a bar slinging the word "sheesh" around like a vocal lasso;

ever lost a bet to a hard boiled detective with a drinking problem, thought about

throwing a lit zippo into the trash under the barely perceptible gutter; ever longed to

be unembarrassed in public, appreciating the digital masonry, waxing lyrical about

the hypercard brick, the expressionist ivy; if you ever redesigned yourself on m.s paint,

transported by the black diamonds in their shading, the earnest fire escapes leading up

to their roofs; ever spent large pockets of time humanizing the interface, like florence

nightingale in the hospital tents of your desktop; ever grew so tired of being careful

not to antagonise the script, gathered useless items in your inventory; if you ever wrote

inside a notebook where the pages go on and on; ever imagined a background of

unaffordable synth, relied heavily on silence to tell the story you could not; i'm a foley

artist telling you i love you using non-human sounds.

---

2. 'Caper in the Castro' was the world's first LGBTQ+ video game developed by C.M Ralph
and released in 1989.

November

II. WHAT'S THIS AFFECT CURVATURE? [BINARISED MOMENTS]

Before carrying away occurs with this distrusted pep, take a breath;

Inhale deep and remember the reliables: it will pose; it will posture; it will plea-away

Noisily towards its binary shadow; dance off to tremble-slump in hrrumph.

Attention all you similar sentiments! A long life understood in rasps of un-surprise

Retrospects 'real-y' if you'll pause, brief. Never irritate to instil the will to

Idle just before committing to accepting this weird happy stance. Be braver.

'Seeming' is the prefix-caveat when entering conviction and Trust Zones.

Each of these skimpy states require atemporal briefing; dossiers to decode.

Denizen-dwellers of drole-land will get it, materialising in material knowledge.

Momentary discomfit results, but better to return to breved and breathable baselines.

Odd feelings of filling scores with temperament suppressors, candour expressors.

Mime-staving the moment with *as if* performances are safety-sutures, but

Easily denuded are these after the shame-walk to next-up-sies and regretitude.

Nervefully face down the urge to call, text or offer up the un-editable when faced;

Tease not the un-suspect public with riff-splays of faux-fuss and anagnorisis.

Stoop, instead, before the semi-pleasure of foreknowledge that dis-ease is dictum.

RETRO-CODING THE MACHINE: IN PRAISE OF SEMI-STRANGERS

it's 'outreach' reaching outward

maybe 'overreach' or overshare to

publicly bare and brace the praise

i like this contra-expectation flies not

the altercations of attitude-alteration decry

from each angle including barbed self-haggle

to like without incite; this is not a question

more a questing gesture of friendly gestation

tough to be so tied up in tumults of 'whys'

but these stamps are social etiquettes uncoded

cryptically forged in the smithies of somethings

called collective assumptions or presumptions

where's the rule book? Autie asking, here!

otherwise smother with sighs and simper

the will at the joys & surprise vicarious-imbibe

from a distantly enabled implement of proximity

strange it is to be in wonder and to wonder

whether one is a personhood-plunderer

of the image-confection in putative public

or list in the inattention of diremption

II *WARM BODIES*

Caustic structures corrode conviviality, or the common strive for such.

Cancerous Visions metastasise through Methods seeming to Strengthen.

Rudimentary Business Principles of anti-knowledge coalesce as cess-

Success semblance, crude clots coagulating around Convenient costs.

Zombies pivot pluck and point to Protocols of appointment rollcalls,

Mirroring maws and muzzles always already prepped for plasmic Exchange.

Centres of power are Asseted through the Strategic sanguinity of blood-let,

Exploited enervation oozes, Emergencied with Efficiency bombs.

Compliance is cathected to chitterlings so the toxicity pools Resources

In Branded tote bags as ready-meat portions, flesh-pounds of hardly paid,

For Participants, Prospects, Customer and Consumer spongy munch.

Such stuff like the liver and lights of academic hides are Served up

And voted with rump and lump sums for Performance slices.

Endemic, acerbic, acidic, corrosive Culture Clashes grume greetings

– no culture clash when monogenean mono-Cultures are teleological,

Enculturation is, *viz*, mono-tropic in-culturation of cruor cephalic –

Tell-tale toxicities of Exchange de-values, the tell-all telegraphed

Signals to phrasal pith retinues proud in pate and Hierarchy-signed.

Alienated in the everyday maw of Maximalised Minimalisation,

The becoming un-dead cling to Unionised gestures of Liquidarity.

Un-dead-itude in all hand-bops & sour coffee & haemo-coeler moments;

Corridor bants, Corpus Christi Bonusses, heads bowed for Armistice;

Gifts of un-hygienic displays of masked hygiene in the Liberty Library;

Hot Spaces vacated to vacuity for perch of other half-bitten bums.

The serum-dripping Sanction to sip the tar-black bile of Private mugshots.

The Poster Presentations of the Demon-strable Will of *Being Well*.

HE DREAMED HE BURST BALLOONS

He dreamed he burst balloons for a living

and was his own supervisor.

He worked twelve hours a week, made a good wage.

He was never exhausted, never bored.

He was calm like a cat full of tuna,

calm like a yacht in a sunlit harbour.

His past life had been forgotten

like a dull episode of a cop show.

There were no scars on his body.

I WAS AN UNARMED TEENAGER

Sunday morning, just after nine

or just before, and the Salvation Army band

strike up a dirge

right under the window.

I roll my hangover

from one red eye to the other, sit up

and stare down at the musicians

in their uniforms, rasping

their dirty hankie tune-

I shoot them

through their mouthpieces

with an imaginary gun.

My mother's getting warm

in front of an open oven,

a pot of tea just made,

Sunday People on the table

open at the crossword page,

and the dog slobbers toward me

with prisoner's eyes

but he's no chance

of a walk on the canal bank

right now. 'How do you die

like a cowboy,' my mother asks,

"four-three-four?"

CHRISTMAS SHOPPING

You were writing dud cheques

like no one's business,

I was splashing

the forged tenners around.

In the hole in the road

someone sang

'Take Me to Tulsa',

snow settling on his sombrero.

I tossed him a tenner

screwed into a ball.

A woman approached

armed with documents

and truth;

she was selling badges,

a definite bargain

at a tenner apiece.

I signed the petition

to end the war,

I do a lot

of possibly useless writing.

WHEN THEY ASK YOU WHERE YOU ARE (REALLY) FROM

Tell them

you are an unrequited pilgrim

two parallel lives that never touch

a whisper or a window

to what your country could be

if only it opened its arms

and took you whole

tell them about the moon

how she eats at your skin

watches you pray and fast and cry

while the world sleeps

how she gives birth to herself and dies

and you wish upon her children

how you wander her night

plant cardamom in your friends' eyes

cumin in their teeth

zaatar on their brow

lick the rest off your fingertips

it tastes of visa-on-entry

heaven with no random checks

round the iftar table everyone speaks

of politics and God

trans rights and colonialism

we forget we didn't speak the empire's tongue

once

THERE ARE BOMBS OVER GAZA AGAIN, ARE YOU WATCHING?

I don't like the post even though I'm tagged

in it, today I am witless on a bus to meet a soul

mate who isn't, in the most liveable city that

isn't, wearing Nikes despite my best intentions

hey, they're anti-Trump but pro-sweatshops, it's

five o'clock and I'm on the wrong bus home, the

cars pile up to flee the free market's spleen, thank

god it's Friday but the bombs are still dropping

on a Palestine that isn't, I am a reporter but feel

silent, making news about house prices and a US

president that isn't, talking about a Muslim ban

that isn't, I am a Muslim on a bus leaving Auckland

and I'm trying not to read the news, talk to friends

in Denver who pray in terminals not made for our

skin and I tweet about Kanye and check my follows

check my new shoes in the glass waiting for the

wrong bus, I wear Palestinian colours by accident

and no one notices, wear a beard by accident

and hope I don't have to travel soon, watch the

skyline shrink and thank god for a hot meal

and Netflix, for a soulmate at a bus stop in a home that

isn't, I don't think about Israeli jets ruffling the nights

feathers, I don't think about when my life is ending

I don't think about where I'll meet my soulmate

if my house is bombed, if my car explodes, if they build

walls in our living rooms and we have to hold hands

through the cracks, if we never see each other again

because of a security policy, though a part of me wonders

if it would make breaking up easier

ON ACCOUNT OF HIS RECURRING DREAM

It began with him digging, spade in both hands,

head down, arms piston-regular, focused.

Why he was doing this and who would cover over

the hole, was never fully questioned.

An internal logic was at work that made this normal.

There was no reason to feel he hadn't known

this was the right time to be digging

or that he hadn't made the most of things.

The location was familiar. He didn't know

how he had arrived at this place but he had a hunch

he could find it on a map. There were signifiers.

It was a place where thistles and hemlock grew.

When the ground was opened-up to the size of a calf,

he put down his spade and lay face up in the hole.

Briefly, the sky became his only view.

In the half-light, earth filled the gap between

his sides, the space above. He tightened himself,

each muscle, taking the extra weight upon his chest,

his arms, his legs, his face, until there was nothing,

just darkness, and the last inhale of stale air

held deep inside his throat was all he had to keep.

THE VOICE

The voice that reads your finest work could almost be your own.

The way it holds each vowel and consonant, the way it softens

at vital moments, lilts, then shifts. This is more distinguished

than the low growling intonation you apply when well-oiled.

The voice is behind a screen behind a screen. Why no face?

Once you were the only source for *you*, or at least you thought so.

Now you're superseded by your upgrade; dare we say, *bettered*.

The voice's program has finessed its algorithm, advanced its code.

The voice adds gravitas, new words in places. Supplanted

by its dulcet tones, you search for your next creative *masterpiece*.

Even that could be pre-empted by the brain of the machine,

that scans and glides across the digital ether, plucking anapaests.

You were merely one input. Your impact on the scene was minimal.

Your ego is tracked and monitored even in sleep mode.

The analytics record you as a footnote in a minor publication,

credit you for turning-up in an age when turning-up was relevant.

CIRCADIAN

A sudden upsurge, a dense murmuration

changing volume against a shapeshifting sky.

Is this an ending or the start of something?

The last bus takes you out to the coast.

You are lulled by its engine beneath your seat,

the intoxicating warmth and engine purr.

Hares beat their way up banks, burrow bound.

Trees tap and scrape the window glass.

The driver presses on, at speed, regardless

until the bus stops and the doors fling open.

Left by only a field, a track, you make your way.

Old rain seeps deep into your boots.

The outline of the guesthouse seems familiar,

as you finally approach. You feel the onrush

of heat as you enter and say your full name.

You'll wake to a single note of silence

that will fill up the room, as if intended to hold,

to pause everything in that one moment.

At which point, the world will break back in

with footsteps, early morning hushed voices,

the same flock resetting into their places again.

DEY CALL AM GRIEF

ma head don scatter

ezigbo scatter

i think na dream be dis

na so e dey be

di tin hapun two weeks before

I don reach fifty

imagine di sadness

dis life

no fit love person

i no get papa again

how person just die laidat

WAHALA DEY

dem carry im body from Accra to Aro Chukwu

the tin no dey easy, for where?

by ambulance dem transport im through

closed borders, Cotonou and Togo

> *n'ime afọ nke ndụ a, jikere maka ndụ ọzọ*

> in di womb of dis life, prepare for di next

dem come bring list, no be one ooooo

first clan, then family bring plenti list:

alcoholic spirits, meat, kola nut, and rice

go fill coolers - ma friend, no be small tin

> *n'afọ nke ndụ a, jikere maka ndụ ọzọ*

> in di womb of dis life, prepare for di next

dem prepare church service, di Cathedral pipo,

dem tok na special programme for distinguished

Maazi, booklet come full thirty pages or so,

hymns and choruses in English and Igbo

> *n'afọ nke ndụ a, jikere maka ndụ ọzọ*

> in di womb of dis life, prepare for di next

dem tok dat church no go bury before clan

dey satisfied, no be small money dis wahala

di kain suitcase-load of naira we carry

use to bury ma dear papa, nwa Atani

n'afọ nke ndụ a, jikere maka ndụ ọzọ

in di womb of dis life, prepare for di next

e be like sey di customs of ma pipo

go finish us sef, threaten put ma broken body

for di same ground with ma papa,

but wetin we go do, sabi no be our culture?

December

METHODOLOGY OF DISPATCH

It lurches, this malnourished place, our warm breath
damp against its tempered glass. Illegitimate symbols
of prosperity fill the swamps where in deepest night
our pallid children set their feet. At Candlemas huddled
between bricks, cherished items gripped with fervour,
paid for with subcutaneous fats, skin, chipped teeth, the
music asphyxiated, drowned by a treble cleft asphalt
reflection. As taillights weep and fade, winter's viscosity
falls quietly at the borders to all but the firm choke of
a young throat. *Home.* The word is mangled. A bloody
incantation conjured from the glossy innards of nation
states so pudding thick and desperate for war business.
Within these midnight places of dispatch, a dove grips
a blade between its beak. Grass, a slip of yellowed plastic.
A jacket daubed with the remnants of inner space or
a buoyant soul. And *still* impotent men button up them
shirts. Damp earth to cover up Dante's hot mouth as
they chew the edge of Sunday's tender lamb. How deceit
is reduced. *A governance of vampires is too crude* I said,
and evil can be grown in the blueish lamplight of each
advantageous house, gardens strewn with wildflowers
ready to bloom, rhizomes hooked within an oesophagus.

THE DAY VENTURE CAPITALISTS REMOVED LIGHT AS A FREE PUBLIC HEALTH BENEFIT

Transactions of the sun knotted into the coat of each family dog. How they pushed the orange rays through the wiry pelt, a brief warmth when pitched against windless repetitions of rotten oath, of ownership. To share in the apprehensive dusk of private garrisons trigger happy for bursts of sharp surprise. Even so, a wonderful peace in the going about of things, the settling down of a nesting dove. The breakage of a mirror helped into the stomach of a gulping litterbin. Laughter coalesced in gutters, cherished toys, our memories pushed around for loose change. *It faded to a pinhole as they dragged it away.* We monitored the temperature of our cooling bodies, talked of sea swimming, the silence of good food. The birds roosted in the chestnut trees; the air felt dense in its blue exaggeration. *'Moonless night'* I heard you whisper. The expression on her face never changed as we held each other in our fragile arms.

MIGRATING FROM AN OPEN WINDOW

A square of down just wanting to rest its bitten

corners and moistened for the chewing palette.

Enduring sleep, a body floats atop its own black

lake as fuel to halt the moons silver sword or the

dullness of an egg tooth tapping its way across an

abstraction of murdered night. To be lost amidst

adolescence, slipped between the pages of a book

written for silhouettes of a future self. Symbioses

held gently as an orb, as proof of the hatching of

another life worth living, not the black carbon of

a birdwing. All freedom is reduced to dust as we

rise up from cracked palms to escape into the sun.

THE WHITE ROOM *MEDUSA*

This is a square, empty room in which there is one window. You can't see a door and you have no idea how you got in. The window is too small to have entered through. You are not in your usual clothes but it's not in a straitjacket either. You find no relief in this. You are frozen against the floor. The floor is strangely soft but provides you with no comfort. This is a clinical space and not the type of hospital you have been forced to stay in. For a moment you think it is no different to White Cube. This isn't a hospital. This is not an experiment. You are part of an exhibition. You are the exhibition. All eyes are on you and you must perform.

It would be something not to perform. It would be something to lie here perfectly still and immobile, both in body and mind. You would not think about solitary confinement. You would not recite poetry in your head. You would not try to count time. You would not try to stay sane. How different would it be from outside of these walls really?

Don't think about what you might have done to end up here. Focus on that window and its perfect, crisp shape. There is life outside. There are laws of nature. The weakest gets killed off, devoured. What is left of its flesh is left to rot. There are anemones, daisies and roses. Think of all those lush blooms which are productive, even in their decay. In their decay, they are fed from. They nourish the earth. The worms feed off them. Seeds take hold. Seeds take root.

THE TITANIC

Out of history they landed the ship's hulk in the earth: straight up from the ground.

Again it comes down to how many people – and when they say 'people', you know –

they can shut in, when death comes reaching. Steerage, in Kensington.

Consider Captain Smith. There were those around him who said 'He went silent,

can you imagine it? Silent!' Captain Smith who, once on deck, knew that it had been

required that lifeboats be removed – a matter of aesthetics – from the First Class promenade.

Smith, who knew the popular chorus: 'Every ship should be her own lifeboat', which

over a century later still reads as 'Just stay put'. Take a further drink. Go back inside,

for the cold outside is dangerous. Stay where you are. They are coming.

Now excuse with ease an absence of effort to move those praying as their kneeling tilts:

Who would deny them their only comfort? What kind of man interrupts prayers?

The purest water came to them, and the waters of ablution always shock the saved.

A Catholic school of thought would still propose, one hundred and five years later,

that 'Common sense' should be enough to lead people from the fire, and such a school

would read the line between Common sense and Common as applied to steerage.

God should be neither questioned nor elbowed away, besides: what life had they?

Something about that Commonality, when handed down, apparently dies

in the passage of fire. So much of that Common is engulfed by fire and flame.

We come in from over the Westway into London swerving in and out

of sightlines, and then the Titanic rises up, in Kensington, before our eyes

in lifeboats of another gilt. Burnt, bodied, still fucking there. It silences the air around.

HYPATIA OF ALEXANDRIA
For Yvonne Reddick

In my telling, she is standing as she might have chosen on the sand beside the sea,

with the tip of her right index finger pressed to her right thumb

and that scope held up to her eye with the stars beyond, contained, within.

And while she knows that so much lies therein that cannot be so simply caught

she is happy that at least as much as she has worked out works,

is there, before her.

In my telling, though she would not have known it, there's a parallel

between what she is doing and what, a small way on, Sigurd would do,

when asked. He held a solar stone up to the dark and was able to locate the sun.

And while, for both, violence was coming, the sky and all its education

was enough for those moments.

In my telling, she turns her lens and narrows an eye and sees raging men,

and the O of her fingers turns bloody and dark, and the sky disappears.

In my telling, she remains on the shore, and the ellipsis that would not kill Copernicus,

nor butcher Galileo, is in the imperfect ring that she has made with our fingers.

And if she thinks of the burning library, it is as nothing to this.

In my telling, she has seen the route, and as she leaves the beach

there is only what she alone can assess

and what we have remembered,

that one day will be termed *in a blade of grass,*

though she smiles that now

it is in her hand.

BACK OFF AGAIN

'I'm sorry that this is so late –

I've never been good

with computers,

You've always been better at

getting things done.'

Having received this from you via email

I held back

congratulations.

I've no idea what about you

you enshrine in technophobia –

what purity you clearly think

such wireless sloth imbues.

Cain picked up the rock as he found it, so,

could we not do this again.

My partner is teaching me to swim.

Or rather, she is helping my body to remember, guiding me back to the water. As a child, I spent whole summers at the local pool, turning somersaults, timing myself to hold my breath, diving for plastic toys on the bottom. But in the years since, I've got out of the habit. Work, sleep, and hoovering have snuck up on me, and I've let my water muscles forget – till swimming has become an unpractised language. A forgotten tongue. I'm loath to be out of my depth. I've developed a terror of getting water on my face, and the thought of putting my whole head under has me heaving fat panicked tears.

And yet – part of me still wants this. I miss that easy movement through a second element, with its lessened gravity. I miss the muscle-knowledge; I'm sure it must lie dormant in my body.

In our first lesson, my partner, L, kicks straight out across the pool. A low sun streams through smeachy windows. Outside, two teenagers sneak a quick cigarette. I walk on tiptoes, arms hugged across my chest. The chill rises up my stomach, needles in at the ribs.

I dip my face into the water – panic and gasp. Water pushes at my nostrils. It scours my mouth, rasping and abrasive. Water as a form of aggression. Water as something to be overcome. I focus so tightly on not breathing in, I forget to breathe out – so the air catches and clogs like a sob at the back of my throat. It's basic human instinct: hold onto your breath in a breathless world. Panic at lack of air.

L takes my hands and guides me across the rippling surface. Gently – gently – she breathes with me:

So let's start with depth. With floating.

First one foot, then the other, I unlock myself from the small blue tiles, tread water, recover old ground.

I try swimming lengths with my head on one side, so I can keep my face above the surface, dip just one ear into the water – as if that might be enough to translate its unfamiliar tongue. I swim. I listen. I try to understand. The voice of the pool is that of an organism: shifting liquid cells, cavernous heartbeat – which is, of course, only an amplification of my own. For the first time in years, I feel this whispered urge to slip my whole head under, to let the water surround me, soft as a pillow. Go on, the water whispers. Come in… My body resists.

After, my stomach is an undertow, my skin a sack of craving. I feel like I could eat for days.

CALEDONIA

200 million years ago, I read

Scotland had been a desert.

Then I left forever that Caledonia,

A country become a land looking backwards,

A sentimental song sketched on a beer mat on a beach

Sure enough, as we fly over

The filigree fingerling fjords of the Forth,

My old home is no more.

The friendly clearances – and mum's departure – have seen to that,

Even though I recognize my old da,

A different man, but still an anchor to the harbour below.

On the edge of the new old world, I am scared.

Over 16 years, I traversed the old new world,

And by the time I was through,

We were an entirely new group of people.

I am changed, too —

My sandstone heart broken, yet held together by succulent American oak.

So, as I survey this new land, I have strength.

You brought me back from Buckie,

And, my Charon, you sailed me safely across the Styx

So I returned from the underworld alive

Even though I had no coin for you, and owe you everything.

Now, as we stand shoulder to shoulder on this remote peninsula,

Scotland may be gone,

But this Caledonia is my adventure with you.

MOONBEAMS

It's morning, the dark's behind us
Thrushes thunder morning chorus
Millions of tons — exploding sun —
Silently stalk the horizon
I want to get closer and hear
But a vast stone blanket of sky
Muffles furious life and fear
Below where the little birds fly
Nothing can be the same again
Touching her each night in my dreams
I had that long curve in my hand
Standing in the spring of moonbeams

And I want to be your Leika
At the edge, falling forever
And orbiting just like Yuri
Beyond the human boundary
Pierce that thick corporeal veil
Once around, two, three, and then
Returning from the celestial
What comes after you've been John Glenn?

Mercury escorts Larunda
With love of glistening quicksilver
Makes way for Leucothea's beau
Bringer of plague, proud Apollo

But being a mortal Apollo

Who sees the long curve of the Earth

Has the hardest act to follow

With no need to prove any worth

So I choose not the lunar leap

Years of fiery climb, descent deep

Instead I prove manly mettle

Skipping straight to Aldrin's bottle

Nothing can be the same again

Touching her each night in my dreams

I had that long curve in my hand

Standing in the spring of moonbeams

VICIOUS

I can feign love: the posture,

the morning caresses, the interlocked walk

down Woodstock Road when it's cold.

It wasn't always so.

*

You were the resurrection of feeling.

Pole raising, flag bearing.

And you said, "There is no direct line

from antiquity to us," as we walked

through a gorge in central Crete.

But I read Hellenistic images into you:

geometric patterns on ancient vases,

red waistcoats, embroidered doilies,

the stickiness of preserved fig.

In this heart of Greece,

a branch swept us into the sun, into

chirruping August. There we recoiled,

grew burnt, hard like day-old bread.

Perhaps you couldn't bear the close scrutiny

of epsilon, olive, and Ypsilantis,

the accusative case.

We became a folktale,

where I tell the story of you, of us, always.

*

Do you wake in the pit of Heraklion's morning

wishing you weren't around,

or that I was around, that the world

was less hostile and you could reach out your arm

to find me curled up on the edge of the bed?

Now that I have loved you,

nothing is near the same.

WORLD'S EDGE

Our love was like a canvas shelter,

provisional, dismantled

in the wake of winter.

At Seitan Limania, we

trekked down to the beach,

invisible from the cliff above.

We made camp at dusk,

cooked rice and beans,

sliced pomegranates,

picked out the pips,

told stories of the netherworld.

Your imagination

charged my desire,

made me want you always.

While you slept, just beyond

my hand's reach,

I got up to watch the blackened sea.

The rocks, vertical, near-human,

caught in the moment before life.

ONE: HARNESS ON A MAN'S THICK FIRM FIGURE

Reins apart, Harvey Holford loved his stirrups.

Christine Holford was holding forward, only to reach

the open street of smiling girls in sledges. Her body:

too heavy for the tow with absolutely no risk.

Come swung lightly as quiver

was used tightly with her feet first time,

her facial defects squared. She felt

balanced ground. She could fool all the way,

this time of day, sporting friends.

Passing the night club, Christine stumbled

for a living creature. Her love smiled,

her breast tanned, harmony assured.

Holford had everything across his face,

curves of clouds on the slopes. He turned grey.

Marvellous snow-covered artificial summits,

the wind skating! Fleece-grace: Holford's

trot thrill! They went, feeling into confidence.

Her muscles met heavy sledges. Faces sat on voice-time.

Christine called this happiness. Christine

from inside already told the noble roadway

her balance. Rhythm stopped thinking.

The rhythm of herself ruled. Her body

was no longer impetuous:

'I see Holford made one happy swing.'

The road couldn't make it, half buried

in an icy trickle down her standing up.

Christine ended ignoring Holford.

They pulled a rest. He suggested being shown

to place, scrubbed and scrubbed his own

character. 'You can breathe in everything.

The people say you love me for my voice.'

With his lips, the waitress disappeared rapidly,

brushed her cheese.

Hungry gorge turns the fragile halo's perched

spindles: a startlingly black waistcoat.

'The females know perfectly well when you scowl.

Darling, I love Harvey.' Christine could see all

the moods that touched her snowball chuck.

His mouth replied in a fierce battle. In the face

they were embroiled, the embarrassed smile.

A somewhat motherly Christine remounted him.

Their lungs occupied adjoining rooms.

'Have a good shivering,' she cried, 'rub a little instinct.'

Sharp, as if it had come from solicitude,

Christine felt cold. Cheeks burning impatiently,

she went, 'That was a beautiful black body.'

Holford moulded her firm: stood, kissed,

stroked her gesture-head. The young woman

spotted Heather Thatcher, her vivacious Viennese

friend, bursting with surgeon-affection for Christine:

'I'm over Germans, our horse took a lovely blue cocktail.'

'English feels foreign,' Holford said, coming back.

'You want a drink, Bloom?' Champagne minds murmured.

John Bloom kissed Heather's touch.

Christine's disagreeable face on his admired fingers,

pleasant enough, endowed with heavenly immobility.

Watch the others think without a skating daresay.

Voice his features, captivate his musical power:

'Girls! Half a dozen. No, just the one! A big Danish!'

'*Scarf!*' squawked Christine, hips like Holford. A

naked look, a jersey besides. He touched his fine

clothes, chilly hands purely erotic, obscene.

Bloom chaste women. 'What made the beauties

of our bad taste?' *His* words (in other words).

PROSE

I: *To the Place of Trumpets*

B rigit Pegeen Kelly was both a rarity and a mystery in late 20th-century and early 21st-century American poetry. A rarity in that she was one of our best and most-admired poets, one of eight poets in any era I wouldn't want to live without, often leading that group. Living poets, or the poets I know, generally speak of her with awe and a hushed reverence, as though the mere mention of her work were something to humble oneself before. That rarified, that rare. Kelly was also a mystery, in that she was a deeply private person, shunning interviews and literary limelight to the point that her body of work, rather than her person, is the figure we've come to know. Perhaps that's as it should be, given the depth of her achievement—its fearsome wonderment, its small but explosive force. She was a rarity, in that every poet I ever met who read her work at length was hooked, and a mystery, in that there's a dearth of scholarship on her work, a chasm of written affection, which this essay seeks in some small part to correct.

Her poems, too, are a rarity, in that they have the power to forever mark their readers, and a mystery, in that the way they mark one can be deeply uncomfortable, unsettling, a taste of something one isn't sure it was safe to imbibe, a sense that the world we see isn't the world we thought we saw. Again, as it should be, since playing it safe is how artists wallow in mediocrity, and how we ourselves tend to circle old fields of habit, blissfully and pitifully blind to the riches of perception we might experience if we stepped not just outside of our comfort zone, but deep into the woods, where the illusion of human dominance drops away, where our strangeness is made self-evident and anything might happen. By *anything*, I mean a human might crawl out of the mouth of a dog, only to do a dance that animates an ancient statue, then crawl back into the dog and continue on their strange, multi-minded journey, wandering into something far beyond human experience, far beyond words and the province of intellectual understanding.

Given the intensity of Kelly's privacy, few biographical details are readily found: born in Palo Alto, California in 1951; died in Urbana-Champaign, Illinois in October, 2016; grew up in southern Indiana; had Irish-American heritage and turned as a teenager towards a Catholic faith;[1] received early training in the visual arts; earned her MFA at the University of Oregon; taught at various universities, settling at the University of Illinois at Urbana-Champaign, where she lived and taught alongside her husband, the poet and writer Michael David Madonick.[2] She had three children, seems to have been widely beloved by her students, cited as being extremely generous with her attention—spending, on occasion, hours discussing a feather[3]—and produced a modest output of three collections of poetry between 1987 and 2004. Except that those books were anything but modest. They were more like little bombs in the forms of books waiting for you to crack them open and light the fuse with your unsuspecting eyes. Critics and prize committees agreed, awarding her the Discovery/ *The Nation* Poetry Prize (1986), the Yale Younger Poets Award (1987), the Lamont Poetry Prize (1994), a Whiting Award (1996), the Witter Byner Poetry Prize (1999),

1. Plumepoetry.com, https://plumepoetry.com/uncovering-what-is-brave-a-remem-brance-of-brigit-pegeen-kelly-by-joy-manesiotis-and-maxine-scates/, accessed December 31, 2024.
2. Enotes.com, https://www.enotes.com/topics/brigit-pegeen-kelly, accessed May 25th, 2019.
3. Michael Minucci, *Dual: Poems*, "On Brigit Pegeen Kelly," Acre Books (2023), 55.

an NEA Fellowship (2005), a Guggenheim Fellowship (2006), and a Fellowship of the Academy of American poets (2008), among others. Her last book, *The Orchard*, was a finalist for the LA Times Book Award, the National Book Critics' Circle Award and the Pulitzer Prize. Had she kept writing at the standard she'd set (or better), I'm certain she would have brought home the lot. But none of that seemed to matter to her, or to matter far less than it did to most. What mattered was the work, and in poem after poem, it shows.

Kelly published her first volume, *To the Place of Trumpets* (Yale University Press, 1988), at the age of thirty-seven. Selected by James Merrill for the Yale Series of Younger Poets, it weighed in at thirty-one poems and seventy pages. In it, she revealed some of the trademark tendencies that would remain central to her work: a mythic and forceful imagination; an obsession with flora and fauna, especially birds, deer, lions, cows and flowers; a fabulist tone and diction that seemed half wrought from an old porch-side storyteller, half contracted from a hermetic oracle; a talent for arresting similes and metaphors; an ear for inconspicuous rhythm that entrances with a steady and incantatory momentum; an affinity for darkness, danger and death; a sense of suffering and pleasure entwined, struggling for dominance, the struggle itself a kind of balance; an aversion to technology and the illusion of the over-empowered human; a simultaneously restrained and rhapsodic rhetoric. Most of all, she displayed an unusual and interesting mind, a mind whose habits of thinking and marveling might transform one's own.

In his introduction, Merrill said, "at the simplest level, she retains the wild, transforming eye of childhood,"[4] which is to say she hadn't dulled her capacity for wonder, nor was her wonder more full of roses than the bodies one might find beneath them. He also noted the presence of her Catholic background, the rituals and iconography which some critics say give Catholic artists a leg up on their Protestant or secular peers, but he rightly noted that she wasn't writing in service of religion. She didn't allow any hold it may have had upon her imagination to confine her art.

---

4. Brigit Pegeen Kelly, *To the Place of Trumpets*, Yale University Press (1988), *ix*.

Note #1

Once upon a time I was born and then I was dying.

Umbilical cord around my neck, it looked like an early exit from a brief life.

But then I wasn't. The doctor sorted me out. I was being dramatic. But I was a baby so that's to be expected. My tongue was tied, but otherwise I seemed grand. Just a very un-notable baby in quite an extraordinary world. Classic case of hurtling into existence.

I was a shy boy. I got embarrassed quite easily. I was afraid to talk to people I didn't know. And at the beginning you don't know almost everyone. But with people I knew and was comfortable with, I was very open. My brother was my best friend and my worst enemy all rolled into one tiny, blonde person. My mother and father were dead on. They gave me food and a bed and toys the entire way up.

As I got older, I got less shy but more fat. I ate a lot. I loved sweets, hated cheese, and enjoyed everything else in between. I was plump. It was described as puppy fat, being big boned. Something I'd grow out of. Which made sense as I'd grown into it. But that was my own doing, so I concluded that I'd have to be the one to instigate the growing-out-of too. I hated most sports. Didn't understand them. That was, until I found basketball and thought it was the most perfect sport anyone could ever play. Once that happened, I started the growing-out-of process. I got taller and less fat— although I'd forever consider myself to be fat afterwards because I had come to believe that I could never not be fat. I grew into my ears that were, up until then, bizarrely disproportionate to the rest of my head.

Girls didn't like me for a long time but then, at some stage, they did start liking me. I was out of the universal friendzone. This was knowledge that changed me. The shyness all but gone, at sixteen I was dating. And then I got my heartbroken. And then my best friend killed himself.

And then I was stuck for the first time really, bar a few micro-moments prior to that. I got stuck. Depressed and untrusting. I wouldn't open up to anyone in any real way for probably another ten years after that. I was seventeen. My route into stuckness was severe and traumatic.

I was emotionally numb for five years. Five years of emotionless, painless, lifeless fun. I tried lots of things to jump start my emotions.

I had a lot of sex. That never worked. I always thought the next time would be different but I always came away feeling nothing but tired, empty. And my partners couldn't understand it because I didn't understand it enough to communicate it effectively. So they left. And I knew I should have felt upset about that but I didn't feel anything. I wanted them to stay while also feeling no way different about their leaving.

I drank. I was in college for most of this stuck part so it didn't appear out of the ordinary. I got on the cans, the pints, the bottles, the whiskey, the vodka. When I was drunk I was able to feel things. It felt nice to feel things. So I got drunk when I could, when my schedule allowed it. Which brings me onto my next point—

I got busy. I played basketball on four different teams. I had two jobs. I was at college. I consumed information, played video games, went on nights out. I did everything I could not to spend time on my own because, if I did that, I'd have to acknowledge that something was off.

I didn't cause myself to become stuck. But I was stuck longer than I had to be because I didn't want to accept it. I dragged it out because I was scared. Scared of feeling broken. Scared of being seen as broken. I could have gotten myself loose long before I did.

But this is the thing about being stuck—when you're in it, you don't have any desire to pull yourself out of it.

Numbness, Anxiety, Anger, Grief

IN the hospital, I am not yet angry. I haven't realised that anger is available to me. And the grief that will eventually hit me is far off still—when someone has survived it is not the time to grieve. In fact, I don't feel as much as you'd think, apart from a sinking sense in my stomach of "this isn't happening again," immediately replaced by a cold brick of, "what do I do now?" I go into problem-solving mode, in which I am not angry at anyone, neither the doctors, nor my mother, nor myself. I am not even anxious, that comes later. Now I am just trying to figure out how to fix my mum.

My mother is in a room in the medical intensive care unit in *Södersjukhuset* in Stockholm. There are four beds in the room, two on each side of a central nurses' station that looks like a space-ship command console with waist-high desks. As I walk in, a nurse in blue scrubs and white clogs is sitting just outside the station, with crossed legs and a kind smile. The room is cosy compared to the general ward I found my mother in last week. My mother, in one of the beds, looks tiny. She is trembling. The smiling nurse gets up and passes me the stool she's been sitting on, while she goes to tend to another patient. I sit next to my mother, and I don't know what to say or how to feel. I do know she was brought here by ambulance in the night after having taken an overdose of antidepressants, because she told me so herself when she called earlier that morning.

I am not yet angry that nobody from the psychiatric ward contacted me when she did this to herself. I am not yet angry that my mother's first suicide attempt was not taken seriously, or that they gave her enough free rein on the ward to allow her to try again. I am not yet angry at the system for not assessing or treating her in any meaningful way after her first attempt, except medically, or at the psychiatric services for merely providing a warehouse for those who harm themselves or others until they are sufficiently pacified by meds or time or boredom to be let out again.

I am not yet angry with my mother. I am not yet angry that she stowed away a hundred tablets of a common antidepressant while she was out on permission with me for the weekend. I am not yet angry that when I then talked to her about the previous suicide attempt a few days before, what she said me made me think that she was persuaded that she could be helped, that we could sort her life out somehow, together. I am not yet angry that she deliberately misled me on the way back to the psychiatric hospital, when she said she was just going to pop into the little corner shop across the road, which was when she hid the meds in some bushes to evade the bag search on admission.

I am not yet angry with myself for being so gullible. I am not yet angry with myself for not realising how bad things had got with my mother. I am not yet angry that there is nothing I can do to help her.

There is a plastic bag on the floor by the bed, with a pair of institutional joggers that I recognise as the ones my mother was wearing the day before. They are stamped with the local psychiatry provider's logo. The trousers are wet, but clean, as if someone has rinsed and wrung them. A wave of sadness and shame washes over me. My mother denies that the joggers are hers. An overdose of SSRIs makes you go into convulsions and fits, so she may not remember. Or she may choose not to remember. It is not the first time I am not sure whether my mother is lying or mistaken. I have often wondered if she changes facts because she needs to, if they then become her truth, or whether she cannot tell the difference, whether her reality is simply not the same as mine.

In a voice still shaking from all the serotonin in her system she tells me that it is her turn to die of depression. That her mother, who lived through the war and brought up two children in post-war communist Poland, died of depression. My grandmother was seventy-nine when she died and now, having turned seventy-four, my mother says it is her turn. That I need to put her in a psychiatric institution or a care home, because that is the way things are going to go.

At least this time around, she recognises me. When I flew in from London a week ago, after her first suicide attempt, she looked at me with confusion and said in a thin, childlike voice, "I promise I will try my best to get better, doctor." I was stunned, it was so not like her, the *her* she was to me: determined and straight-talking. "It's me, mum, your daughter." I vividly remember the red wool jumper I was wearing; I can't put it on without thinking of this moment. It took her a beat, but then I saw realisation in her eyes. I don't recall what we said to each other, but her voice was her own again. The same voice my mother uses now, the second time around in hospital, when she tells me about my grandmother and depression and death.

Before she is discharged back to the psychiatric ward, she is seen by the hospital's on-call psychiatrist. I am asked to attend with her permission. We are in a small room: muted grey walls and muted green upholstery. My mother is in a wheelchair wrapped in a pale-yellow hospital blanket. She repeats what she has told me. What my mother leaves out of the story is that she left her native Poland with her husband and infant at a time when her father was dying of cancer and that she never saw him again, that her mother suffered from dementia for years and lived with my mother's sister and her family in a small flat for many of those years. There are layers of trauma and guilt behind my mother's words, but nobody asks any further questions.

The best the on-call psychiatrist can do is to berate my mother for what she has done to me. "Look how upset your daughter is, you need to be strong so that you don't cause her anymore pain." Even though I don't know then what I have since come to know, this strikes me as the most preposterous thing to say to someone who has just tried to take their own life. You can't guilt someone out of suffering. Even when anger floods me later, wave after wave, I know that my anger is not going to heal my mother. Why isn't anybody asking what brought her here? Why isn't anybody asking why she wants to kill herself? Even now that my anger has turned to profound sadness, I know my grief isn't going to heal her either.

HOPSCOTCH BY JULIO CORTÁZAR

JULIO Cortázar's postmodernist novel *Hopscotch* is a novel of forking paths. On the one hand, you can read chapters 1-56 in order. That way, we follow the story of Horacio Oliveira, an Argentine intellectual slumming it in 1960s Paris. Oliveira is in love with a woman called Lucía, whom he calls 'La Maga' ('The Magician'). We follow their life in Paris. There is a mix of conventional dialogue/action scenes with non-narrative discourse. He, La Maga and their group of bohemian friends from (among other places) Herzegovina and Montevideo hang out in bars and bedrooms, playing jazz records and squabbling existentially with each other. Nothing much happens. And yet everything. The mundanity of everyday life is raised to the level of the sublime and vice versa. So far, so good.

On the other hand, before the novel starts, Cortázar inserts a suggestion to the reader that they should read the novel haphazardly. He issues a 'table of instructions' that requires the reader to hop from chapter to chapter, seemingly without connection. This way, reading the novel is like watching a film whose scenes are edited in the wrong order. When I say 'wrong', I am wrong, of course. There is no 'right' or 'wrong' way to order events. Conventional narrative observes the laws of cause and effect but this sequence places 'consecutiveness' above causality. Things happen in spite of, not because of, what has happened before.

Cortázar's suggestion means that causality becomes a casualty. Set this way, scenes are placed in harsh juxtaposition. Jolted out of our expectations, we lurch from scene to scene, fumbling to make a connection where there is seemingly none. At first, this is bewildering, but at some point, this bewilderment becomes exhilaration. At the end of each section, we have no idea what will happen next. Time and again, we are pulled back to zero. Now, we are walking through the story, not in a straight line, but in Brownian motion. And isn't that a more natural way to experience a place and time? Nature is chaos, not order. We put events into an order so as to understand them – plot them into a story – but life itself is haphazard, isn't it?

Hopscotch is a random amble through the city. Because there's no linear narrative flow, you can dip in and out of the book, never knowing how close or far away you are from the end. An aimless walk, a wander without purpose. It takes time to adjust, but once accepted, it becomes addictive. Cortázar's interest in the layout of Paris bears similarities with Walter Benjamin's *Arcades Project* and André Breton's novel *Nadja*: 'Paris is a centre, you understand, a mandala through which one must pass without dialectics, a labyrinth where pragmatic formulas are of no use except to get lost in.'

Published in Buenos Aires in 1963 (and in English in 1966), Cortázar's novel was written at the height of the postmodern project (interestingly, its aleatory technique was adopted at the same time by composer John Cage, who used the I Ching to compose many of his pieces). His fellow Latin American authors quickly recognised Cortázar's achievement and his novel is now regarded, along with Márquez's *One Hundred Years of Solitude*, as the greatest novel published in the Spanish language since *Don Quixote*. His successor is fellow *enfant terrible* Roberto Bolaño, whose mammoth (and astonishing) novel *2666* (2004) might be read as a homage to Cortázar. Although now more than 60 years old, the play and freedom found in *Hopscotch*, its sense of dislocation and displaced identities, seem astoundingly current. Over those years, *Hopscotch* has not lost its zest for life one jot.

ONE HUNDRED YEARS OF SOLITUDE
BY GABRIEL GARCÍA MÁRQUEZ

The tone that I eventually used in One Hundred Years of Solitude *was based on the way my grandmother used to tell stories. She told things that sounded supernatural and fantastic, but she told them with complete naturalness.*

— Gabriel García Márquez

IT took me four days solid to read this, so transfixed was I. What a book! As Milan Kundera says, 'García Márquez's novel is free imagination itself. One of the greatest works of poetry I know. Every single sentence sparkles with fantasy, every sentence is a surprise, is wonder.' One of the hardest things about the book is keeping track of who's who – there's a lot of slippage. Children are constantly born in and out of wedlock and everyone is somehow related to everyone else. It's a story of contrasts, crossovers and worlds collapsing into each other – living/dead, inside/ outside, past/present, rural/urban, knowledge/ignorance, democracy/totalitarianism. Every event carries equal weight and significance – a life is summarised in a few lines, someone's death is mentioned only in passing, and then the narrative quickly moves on to a much more detailed description of how a house is built. Although the narrative is written as one long monologue, without 'scenes', it's a very 'readerly' book, in that it invites many and various interpretations (my good friend Jason Watkins wrote a paper on it when we were at uni – he got a first) and I can see why – it is so rich in themes/ motifs/imagery (the yellow butterflies!). As another friend, Alex, pointed out, it's also a time-travel book. The similarly-named characters are perpetually born and face the same hardships, prejudices and grudges in their lives, so we get a sense of permanent *déjà-vu*. All the women either die young or live well into old age under a vow of silence and all the men are shot. Such repetition halts the progress of time; time is cyclical, we cover 100 years and yet it goes by – poof – just like that... Like all great novels, it immerses you in its world and shows you how life is. There isn't another book like it in the whole of the world. It stands tall, blocking out the light and casting a huge shadow. Majestic.

EYES IN THE WOOD :
HOW TO KNOW A WORLD WHICH IS ALWAYS
LOOKING BACK?

ON the banks of the River Mersey at Cressington Park esplanade, low tide, sandbanks rising, crows peck along the waterline. I look across to Eastham Ferry on the edge of the Wirral Peninsula, to green woods and a white building, once a hotel, cwtched into the dark trees. The view beyond leans into the Clywdian hills where a brightness frames the distance. Grey clouds balance along the ridge like a scale, hold equilibrium as the river flows towards and in; the sea to the west loosening its grip and the towers of Stanlow oil refinery dragging waves to the east. A hammer taps this shore; a man behind a garden wall, behind me, trims the already-neatened hedge.

I have come here to look back at the old white hotel and meet its gaze. I can see the frontage from every walk I take on this side of the river. I have come here to think about knowing, to write in my recycled notebooks in blue scrawling ink, whatever happens in the act of looking back. I can only do this when I am on the edge of my city, Liverpool. I will tie all the strands together later, on a computer, finding meaning in my improvisations and in that binding action, question and learn. I am trying to describe how I think as a poet and writer; how the knowledge gleaned within being becomes a poem; how a non-linear conception of time and space is not a representation, a false imagining but an engagement with the entanglement of the world. Starting from an ontology which isn't linear or neat requires an atunement to how meanings shift, change and transform within subjectivity and how being presents these to the mind as meaningful: steppingstones within the peat. Poetic thought in practice is an act of stepping sideways, or leaping over decaying branches, or digging through the ground. I have to go around, over and through, down into as I am always within the thought. I can't just count the leaves on the tree or cut it up into tiny pieces whilst feeling powerful about its subservience to my mind and method: O how sharp is my axe. Hubris will lead to false knowledge, parts not systems, dominance understood as truth rather than the defensive act it is. Truth isn't dominant, it is wide-open and more-than-human.

*

To write about looking back I will write about my ancestors. One of my earliest memories, or a memory I've come to name as such, is seeing the 'eyes in the wood', the wood-panelled walls of a Victorian vicarage on the edge of a small post-industrial town in Lancashire. My grandfather was an Anglo-Catholic, Anglo Welsh vicar from a family of four generations of clergy, beginning in South Wales on the Gower Peninsula in the 1840s. I can now see again the exterior in my mind's eye, though my memory is of how the dark wooden interior looked back towards a toddler running from study, to living room, to kitchen in a loop. Each room had connecting doors which enabled this flow. My grandfather peeled an apple in one corkscrew move: no breaks. I have always understood objects as living phenomena, looking back into my gaze.

And raising my eyes again, I meet the white hotel, or the muddy grey, small, tamed presence encircled by trees to its back and the wash of silver to its front. In the Rees family archive of 19th century letters, lectures, drawings and scrapbook is a letter written by Rev. William Davidson Wood-Rees, my great, great grandfather to his mother on the occasion of his honeymoon. I read it in May 2020, and now it is two years later, and only now do I feel I can speak with his thoughts. They have settled in me, fleshed out in images. I intended to quote his words here in this essay, to amplify his words across time. But in practice, in the first draft of this text, I left silences, told myself I just didn't want to risk taking the letter out of the plastic folder in the storage box, risk dirtying its fragile surfaces. I let his voice sing only as placeholder hashtags in the gaps in the sentences and so, from memory, invoke what I have read to reanimate his words in mine.

Do I have my ancestor's permission to quote his words from an intimate letter written to his mother kept quiet in a box for two hundred years, reanimated only by his descendant's eyes, perhaps once a generation? How would I feel if in two hundred years' time my private letters were quoted in public? On reflection, I'd hate it. I felt this recognition as a force, the boundary between private and public, ink and speech, a form. I will not steal Wood-Rees' words, cajole them into my own meanings, but animate them through my body, transform them through my own speech.

*

Wood-Rees is standing on the water's edge, looking back towards me. It is 1879 and he has travelled on the steamer from Liverpool Pierhead landing stage to the pleasure gardens downriver as part of his honeymoon, walking now with his love in the green woods. He sees the training ships in the Mersey and almost sees me looking back at him across the moon-drawn river. Wood-Rees writes about his trip to Eastham Ferry pleasure gardens in his letter to his mother that I read one warm May Day in 2020, unable to go outside due to Covid lockdown. Wood-Rees speaks to me through my astonishment that he also walked the roads I know and write, also crossed the river I've always crossed; that traces of me were here before I came to be; that my memories linger and shiver now, carried in his body, also finding their way into his own life, drawing together here in my gaze at the edge of the river towards Eastham Ferry and the blur of the white hotel.

...You said nothing was worth pursuing, in the end, if it wasn't a case of pleasure. Or did I say that. I said something about growing older. Our conversation looped in ribbons – three shades of green – then stilled around a void. We'd soon enough stop speaking. We were a starlight sugar level. What was in that case? Your mother nurtured white poppies so that every May when the garden darkened all you could see were their pale wee faces, hardening against the dark like eyes. The many-eyed garden of your mother. A space we locked away. I remember kissing you then, close to the edge. The way you tasted milky. That was a pleasure way. How I wanted this bottled. Closer to lilac in the light. Your eyes strained from screens I was kissing you better, kissing them close to sleep. Of course, we hid from your mother, and pretty much everyone else, when we kissed. You poured a glass of milk from the fridge.

There was pleasure, something of the Romantics I read at school: this Wordsworthian thing about pleasure. No one around me could tolerate this level of daffodil crap. As it was, I was hoarding Dorothy's journals and obsessing over her drinking tea, with such constancy it put my old scrolling habits to shame. Break for tea, tea at breakfast. Spill the tea. I've been trying, casually, to make statements of correlation between tea consumption and weather. There was pleasure there. My blood all rich with caffeine, twirling on a spot to make motion of the light in your eyes and speech at the party. Green light tea. It's all gossip. What? Other people speak of the narrative lapse of cigarettes. Okay so it's raining. I'm scrolling. You're typing. There was a rhythm to our quitting, arrangements of sugary negative space. With words we drew a new foreground...

...When all we wanted in the end was to disappear (in one another). The rain became mist, then milky distance. For drawing one sigh is the sound of the other, whose motion you can hardly class as light. At work, when they talked about it, teased us, all I could think of was your breath. I conducted desire in unruly shifts. There could be no fresh release. Was it me, no, would I ever?

"Who *was it* Marlene?"

Mostly I drifted towards the one table where a window let in the afternoon, the sheer fact of its atmosphere. I brought over rusted pots of Twinings Breakfast tea, my fingers dusty from arranging the tablet just so on the side. Hospitality is the trading of one thing for the other, a ceaseless admittance of instability. Here you go. Speech acts for self-erasure. Melt in your mouth.

Nobody knows what they really want. Why think five years or even a meal ahead?

I was not always in this line of business; or as a matter of fact in this, the other.

Your mother, like others, would never know enough to ask what I did.

Shift patterns promote idleness. I fall into one loophole only to catch breath on the start of the next, till the hours slack a lariat of absence around my nervous system. So even as I pace, carrying plates, I say it again I miss you. There's a beat.

Whose? Here I am, still picking at blood flakes in the palm of my hand.

A chef picking chilli flakes from Tesco.

Sometimes, I'm like Emily. It's like Hi, I'm no one! When I write this, who are you?

I had a friend called Emily
and we were so young: we fell
into our respective wardrobes.

What age are we to receive first self-assurances, like appreciate life's big thrust, blood in our veins and everything? When very sapling, a babe on the floor must be approximate; just as gold might be an unseen sun, but it's just the glint of a pound, someone's earring. Lying on the carpet like that, upside down, is really an athletic feat. Pretend you are looking for something, when all this adds up to a defiance of gravity. I collect the words *kidney, alias, shelf, artichoke* & *stones*.

*
**

I don't remember that much from my first day at school. I was intrigued by all the sudden haircuts, styles abounding, strange imitations of pop stars from telly. Nobody had a *haircut* before my first day at school. We didn't watch that kind of television at home. We looked at magazines in the dentist's office. Mum cut our fringes with zig zag scissors because she loved David Bowie. It was the nineties and every boy was a boy in a boy band, at the very least virtually, at the very least as miniatures — those plastic statuettes! Girls with plaits, whose process of elaborate fashioning I'd contemplate like sculptural algebra. I remember mostly the first hour of class, sitting round a table presided over by this kid, a boy shorter than me but with god's own aura about him. Even at five, his face looked wrinkled, as if his birth was the great difficulty of his life from which he would never recover. He kept saying "Aye aye aye aye aye" over and over. I didn't know what Aye meant. I felt glitchy and English. I hated to feel English, but it seemed I'd feel glitchy for the rest of my existence, like somebody forgot to finish my code, so I would never land at Subject. The Aye seemed to emanate power around him. I thought he was saying "I I I I I" and each "I" was like another candle liberally stabbed into the invisible cake he had in front of him, the icing mushing everywhere. Happy birthday to the brand new day. I didn't get it. I mean obviously he was saying yes to something. But in that moment I just thought he was asserting himself, his I-ness, aye sure, over and over. I didn't know you could just take from the room and add a fat chunk of you like that. Someone kicking me hard in the shins. Cherry red mark and shining. A candle to kingdom come.

7 years later, we're still laying out our unrest